Success
guide

HIGHER
Physical Education

Ann Duff ✕ Thomas Hardie

Contents

Introduction

Welcome	4
Getting started	5
Analysis of performance areas	6
Understanding the command words	7
Making the most of this book	9

Analysis Area 1: Performance Appreciation

Quality performance	11
Qualities required for top performance	15
Mental influences on performance	21
Model performers	26
Planning your training	30

Analysis Area 2: Preparation of the Body

How fit are you?	38
Specific fitness needs and role responsibilities	44
Types of fitness	50
Principles and methods of training	55
Planning effective training	62

Analysis Area 3:
Skills and Techniques

Skill and skilled performance 68

Analysing, monitoring and reviewing skills and techniques 75

The three identifiable stages of learning 80

Analysis Area 4:
Structures, Strategies and Composition

Structure and strategy fundamentals 89

Roles and relationships 95

Gathering information to aid decision making 102

Study guide 107

Welcome

As a Higher student you will have embarked upon your physical education course of study first and foremost because you enjoy sport. Secondly, you will have demonstrated a high level of practical performance and will also have been committed to studying your performance from a sports science approach.

Whilst this book is specifically designed to support you by developing the skills, knowledge and examination techniques needed to achieve success, it recognises the importance of linking learning to prior knowledge. Physical Education may be just one of the examinations you are preparing for. You should, therefore, integrate the learning experiences gained from your other subjects as this will help you to:

- consolidate your learning
- refine your reading comprehension
- improve your literacy skills
- challenge your thinking

and most importantly, help you to more fully understand the Physical Education facts that will be tested in your examination.

Many subjects have overlapping core skills demands, for example:

- reading questions
- interpreting questions
- recall of subject information
- applying the subject information in context.

Many subjects require you to:

- describe
- explain
- discuss.

This challenges your ability to demonstrate logical, analytical and critical thinking.

Do not just write in the discipline of Physical Education, but rather write to *learn*. Subjects are not stand-alone so, *think* – make the *link*. This will enrich your appreciation of facts and improve your critical thinking skills.

Getting started

Let us help you make sense of what your Higher Physical Education examination is all about. Understanding what the exam is assessing will help you prepare your answer and achieve success.

Exams are written to discover not only how much of your subject you know but also the associated skills that you are expected to demonstrate. In Physical Education you will be assessed on both your acquired and applied knowledge and understanding of a number of concepts.

This tests your logical, analytical and critical thinking skills by asking you to *describe* facts, often in detail; *explain* facts, often in detail; *discuss* or *justify* facts requiring description, explanation and opinion. Your mark will be based on how effectively you meet these skills.

Throughout your studies you will be taught and will learn a lot of new information. This 'new information' or **key concept** knowledge will be delivered to you in a number of different ways. For example, as you:

- work to develop aspects of your performance
- apply theory to your training/practice development
- complete your internal unit assessment (NAB)
- complete your homework assignments
- complete your private study notes.

Your understanding of **key concept** knowledge is what will be tested in your examination.

Top Tip

Top Tips dotted throughout will help you recognise what you are being asked and importantly what information you must include in your answers to access full marks.

The 2.5 hour question paper is made up of eight questions – two questions are set from each of the four **analysis areas:**

- Performance Appreciation
- Skills and Techniques
- Preparation of the Body
- Structures, Strategies and Composition

You are required to complete three questions each from a different area of analysis. In each area you will have a choice of two questions. Each question is worth 20 marks and is made up of four parts – a), b), c) and d). Each part of the question will reveal the mark value; often a 4- or 6-mark allocation for the knowledge you are expected to demonstrate. Several command words will help you recognise what the question is asking you.

Your question selection will depend on the course structure you have followed. Importantly, you should select the questions you know most about. This requires you to read the whole question to make sure you know what you are being asked. Plan your answer and manage your write-up time. During your course study your teacher will give you plenty of opportunity to practice answering questions.

Studying the following sections in this success guide will help you to gain a fuller understanding of **key concept** knowledge in each of the four analysis areas. You should pay specific attention to the **key concept** information you have studied during your course.

Analysis of performance areas

During your course you will be involved in studying and learning specific knowledge (KEY CONCEPTS) in four analysis areas:

- Performance Appreciation
- Skills and Techniques
- Preparation of the Body
- Structures, Strategies and Composition

This is a quick reference guide that shows you the types of information you will be studying.

As you work through the different areas of analysis in chapters 1–4 you will get greater detail about the related knowledge and guidance to improve your examination technique.

Performance Appreciation

In this area you will learn about:

- how each of the other analysis areas link to give you a full picture about your 'whole performance'
- methods used to collect data and plan/monitor for improvements
- the specific qualities and fitness demands of activities or roles

FACTS

about how to improve your 'whole' performance

- developing skills/techniques
- different strategies, structures and tactics used to be successful in activities.

Skills and Techniques

In this area you will learn about:

- gathering data – identifying your technique strengths and weaknesses
- comparing to model performers
- different types of skills
- developing your skills and techniques via different methods of practice
- stages of learning
- factors that will affect you when you learn and apply your strengths and weaknesses
- how to process information.

Preparation of the Body

In this area you will learn about:

- gathering data – identifying your fitness strengths and weaknesses
- different types of fitness/ fitness testing
- developing your fitness via various training programmes
- principles that will ensure your training is effective
- planning short- and long-term training.

Structures, Strategies and Composition

In this area you will learn about:

- gathering data – identifying your strengths and weaknesses within the role or team
- applying various structures and strategies
- adapting/changing structures and strategies
- how to develop your structures and strategies via different practice or training methods
- factors that will affect you when you apply your structures and strategies
- decision making when applying structures and strategies

FACTS
about how to improve your 'specific parts' of your performance

Understanding the command words

Understanding what type of response the examiner wants requires that you read and analyse the question carefully.

Remember! The question acts as your instructions.

To analyse and interpret the question accurately requires a good knowledge of the meaning of **command words**. **Command words** are your guide as to what knowledge is being targeted by the question. They are used to give you maximum help as to what the examiner is looking for.

The Physical Education exam paper is set in a structured manner with the **command words** used consistently to test your understanding of both acquired and applied knowledge. As you work through the following Analysis of Performance chapters you will consider and work with these command words to increase your confidence at interpreting what is being asked of you. It is best you make sense of these **command words** as these always feature in your exam.

Study carefully the table below. Refer to it as you work through the remaining chapters.

Top Tip

Referring to this regularly will develop your analytical and critical thinking skills.

Top Tip

If you can get a grasp of these **command words** then you are on your way to making coherent connections between theory and application.

COMMAND WORDS	RESPONSE REQUIRED Tell the examiner as much as you know
Describe Describe in detail	Without interpreting the information: • give information • convey a mental picture • give an account
Outline	Brief identification of a point, with a little explanation. Offer the main points.
Identify	Pick out some of the key factors. List or name them.
Analyse	Examine closely. Look at the facts/evidence/data – interpret what you find.
Explain Explain in detail	May require definition or description. Make clear the detail. Think about the *how* and *why* – give reasons.
Suggest	Make a judgement and give examples to support your answer. Decide the value of.
Compare	Point out similarities and differences between one or more factors.
Discuss/Justify	Examine closely taking account of strengths and weaknesses. Value for and against, criticise or appraise in terms of impact or significance to performance development. Offer reasons. Refer to evidence/data. Substantiate your opinion.
Evaluate/Assess	Make judgements, look at the evidence and back up points raised. Substantiate your opinion.

As you study the Analysis of Performance chapters – you will be given specific examples of how these **command words** are used to test your acquired and applied knowledge.

Command words in the exam

Here are some examples of how these **command words** will be used in your Physical Education examination.

- *Describe* the methods of data you used to gather information on your performance.
- *Outline* your strengths and weaknesses when performing in ...
- *Indentify* the qualities you would expect to see in a model performer.
- *Analyse* the information you gathered about your whole performance.
- *Explain* why it is important to monitor your progress.
- *Suggest* why your performance may be more effective during practice than during performance.
- *Discuss/Justify* the factors you took into consideration when ...
- *Evaluate* your results after your training programme is completed.
- *Assess* your ability compared to that of a model performer.

Top Tip

Remember – this simply means recalling the information you have learned and demonstrating you know how to use it to improve your practical performance.

As you work through the remaining chapters you will get guidance on how to answer these types of questions fully to gain maximum marks.

And remember what we said earlier – make the link!

Use your learning experiences gained from the study of your other subjects to help you. For example, which of your other subjects requires you to respond in the same manner?

Use of command words

Think back to the **command word** table – understand what is being asked of you! As you can see from the question examples, the **command words** are used in different contexts. From year to year the examiners will change how they word the questions to test your real understanding of subject facts.

Good exam technique

1. READ the question.
2. NOTE the mark value.
3. CONSIDER the **command word** (this has been embolden for you).
4. REFLECT on what the **command word** is telling you to do.

Making the most of this book

The **analysis area** chapters explain all course information. From the study of a number of **key concepts** *(facts you need to be able to recall)* related to each **analysis area** you will learn how to identify your performance strengths and weaknesses and select and apply methods to bring about improvements in your performance in relation to at least one of the following contexts: individual, team, group, task, skill, technique, fitness, strategy.

Asking yourself the following questions will help you to be logical in your approach and improve your critical thinking skills.

* What is my performance focus?
* What do I need to collect to provide evidence of my performance strengths and weaknesses?
* How will I collect this evidence?
* From my analysis – what does this evidence reveal about performance?
* What training and or practice will best address weaknesses I have prioritised for improvement?
* What will my improved performance look like?
* How will I justify my performance improvement(s)?

In each **analysis area** you will be required to work with many types of data gathering that are *general, initial focussed* or *specific*. This helps you to prioritise which parts of your performance you will attempt to improve. Your logical and critical thinking will become evident depending on your selection.

For detailed information about data gathering purpose and type see page 76–77.

Do not worry you are not expected to know everything in this book! But much of it will impact on your learning. Your teacher will select the most relevant **key concepts** *(related facts)* to match the practical activities taught in your school or college. It is important therefore that you refer to the **analysis areas** you are studying during your course, as this ensures you have the correct knowledge and understanding to help you pass your examination.

From a sports science perspective, reading *all* the chapters in this book will give you the 'bigger picture' and broaden your appreciation of performance development.

The structure

At the end of each **key concept** information section you will be directed to SQA past paper sample answers. To gain the most benefit you will examine discrete question parts *either* a), b), c) or d). This will enable you to focus on the core skill demands of reading questions, interpreting questions, recall of subject information, applying the subject information in context.

You will be given an examiner's opinion on the merits of the sample answer. This will develop your appreciation of how to address the competencies examined of demonstrating logical, analytical and critical thinking.

The **key concept** selected by your teacher will be from the four **analysis areas**. As you work to improve your practical performance you will develop your understanding of these.

Area 1 Performance Appreciation

1. Overall nature and demands of quality performance.
2. Technical, physical, personal and special qualities of performance.
3. Mental factors influencing performance.
4. Use of appropriate model performers.
5. Planning and managing personal performance improvement.

Area 2 Preparation of the Body

1. Fitness assessment in relation to personal performance and the demands of activities.
2. Application of different types of fitness in the development of activity specific performance.
3. Physical, skill-related and mental types of fitness.
4. Principles and methods of training.
5. Planning, implementing and monitoring training.

Area 3 Skills and Techniques

1. The concept of skill and skilled performance.
2. Skill/technique improvement through mechanical analysis or movement analysis or consideration of quality.
3. The development of skill and the refinement of technique.

Area 4 Structures, Strategies and Composition

1. The structure and strategies that are fundamental to activities.
2. Identification of strengths and weaknesses in performance in terms of roles and relationships, formations, group and team principles, tactical or design elements, choreography.
3. Information processing, problem solving and decision making when working with structures and strategies to develop and improve performance.

Quality performance

> **Key concept 1**
> Overall nature and demands of quality performance.

Remember in this **analysis area** you will be studying information that will help you to analyse your **whole** performance. Your **whole** performance incorporates many factors including identification of your strengths and weaknesses, specific qualities, your fitness and skill levels and your ability to be strategically aware.

The knowledge you will acquire from studying this key concept will help you to understand about:

* the nature of different activities
* the specific demands of different activities.

The nature of an activity simply means, 'What makes the activity unique?' The demands of an activity simply mean the physical-, technical-, mental- and skill-related challenges that will be demanded for a performer to be effective.

Badminton

For example, the nature of badminton is that it:

* is an indoor activity
* is played on a regulation court size
* is directly competitive
* is played for leisure or competition
* is played in single, doubles or mixed-doubles contexts
* is played at a high, fast, energetic pace
* has specific scoring systems/codes of etiquette
* is officially classed as the fastest paced racket sport in the world.

For example, the demands of badminton are that it:

* is physically demanding as rallies are fast-paced and the player(s) work-rate must be sustained for the duration of the game; cardio-respiratory, muscular and speed endurance will be tested. Placement of shots will require flexibility and power to ensure disguise and accuracy.
* is technically demanding as attacking and defending skills will be challenged constantly. A range of simple and complex skills must be evident to ensure opponents are out-manoeuvred.
* is mentally demanding as players will require complete concentration with an ability to handle emotions to make appropriate decisions and challenge for every point played.
* is skill-demanding as the player(s) must produce excellent footwork, be balanced and have the agility to cover the court quickly with timing, co-ordination, reaction time evident to anticipate flight path of shuttle.
* is strategically demanding – with different tactics required for singles/doubles play. Players must be able to control rallies with varied tempo and disguise.

Rugby

Let us consider another example, this time a team sport – rugby. For example, the nature of rugby is that it is:

- an outdoor activity – affected by weather conditions
- played on a regulation pitch
- a directly competitive team activity
- controlled by specific rules/codes of conduct
- played in a team of 15 players with named substitutes
- a team sport where every player has specific role-related responsibilities
- played at a high, fast, energetic, aggressive pace
- a game of 80 minutes, with two halves of 40 minutes.

For example, the demands of rugby are that it is:

- physically demanding as scrums, rucks, mauls and line-outs are powerful and aggressive actions and the players work-rate must be sustained for the duration of the game therefore levels of cardio-respiratory, muscular and speed endurance will be tested.
- technically demanding as attacking and defending skills will be challenged constantly, for example, passing, tackling, shooting.
- mentally demanding as players will require complete focus and concentration to challenge for every pass/tackle/move on/off ball. Players must manage emotions and control aggression to avoid giving away penalties or be 'sin binned'.
- skill-demanding as the players must produce great anticipation, reaction time, agility, timing and coordination and balance to be successful in their role within the team.
- strategically demanding depending on role and team plays. Players must have the ability to select, apply and respond to tactical play in response to a) the team's own game plan, b) the opponents' game plan and c) weather conditions.

In your other subjects you may have been challenged to debate your opinion. This means compare and contrast, support the points you make.

Essentially, to be *effective* in any activity relies on your knowledge of not only the specific nature and demands of the activity but of the related demands of specific roles, tactics and fitness.

Remember you may be involved in more than one sport, for example an individual or team activity; or you may be required to play more than one position; or you may be in a position to help others improve their performance.

Top Tip

This knowledge will help you design your training to address your identified weaknesses.

Quick Task

In your opinion would you argue that the demands of an individual activity compared to a team activity are greater?

By preparing your debate you are developing your critical thinking skills.

Summary

Nature and demands

Why has it been important to learn about this key concept?

Learning about this **key concept** has a range of benefits:

1. You will be more knowledgeable about the specific nature and demands of your activity(ies) and about the role you are responsible for within the activity(ies).
2. You will be able to link this understanding to make sense of other **key concepts** as you study the other analysis areas.
3. You will have broadened your appreciation of performance development from a sports science perspective – *simply put* – you will be able to talk/think more knowledgably about a range of issues.

For example, you will be able to consider:

- which training/practice methods would best suit the activity specific demands of your activity
- role related/team responsibilities when planning and applying strategies or preparing game plans
- planning and managing training programmes
- principles of practice/training to ensure programme design is effective.

Using these strategies in the exam

Remember, in your exam you may be required to demonstrate your understanding of this **key concept** by recalling the information. In this instance, you could be asked to:

- describe the nature and demands of your activity
- describe the specific demands of your role within an activity.

Alternatively you could be asked to demonstrate how you were able to make use of this acquired knowledge. For example, you could be asked to:

- explain why it is important to consider the nature and demands of your activity
- explain the specific strengths you have that enable you to perform effectively in your activity
- discuss how you planned your training to meet the demands of the activity
- discuss how your performance was affected as a result of not coping with the specific demands of your activity.

Look back at the commands words on page 9.

 In your other subjects, think about how the **command words** used to test your knowledge of the subject matter in different ways.

Quick Task

Write up the nature and demands of the activity you are most involved in. Keep this as part of your study notes. It will help you to recall information more efficiently.

Improving your exam technique

Let us examine a past paper question and response.

Good exam technique

1. READ the question.
2. NOTE the mark value.
3. CONSIDER the **command word** (this has been embolden for you).
4. REFLECT on what the **command word** is telling you to do.

Sample question, answer and feedback

Question

Chose **one** activity. **Describe** the demands of a **quality performance** within your chosen activity.

4 marks

Now read the sample answer

Note: the description word/phrase has been highlighted in blue.

There are many different demands needed for a quality performance in volleyball. There are the technical demands of this fast-paced rebound game as each team tries to score points quickly. Attacking skills such as, setting, volleying and spiking are needed to keep the rallies going and set up winning opportunities. Defending skills such as blocking and court coverage are needed to prevent the opposition from attacking and ending the rally.

There are physical demands, such as having to cover the court at speed. Power and muscular endurance demands on the legs as there is a constant need to jump high to hit a spike or block at the net. Also there are strong cardio-respiratory demands as I have to last for the full game, often in long tiring rallies.

There are personal demands in that I need to remain focussed and concentrate on all shots played so that I do not let my team down. There is tremendous need to be alert and work co-operatively with my team as the game tempo can change so quickly from me needing to attack one minute and then move back to cover in defence. I also need to be aware of the tactical demands of the game, for example, being aware of my team strategy so that I play my role (setter) well and get into good cover positions; jumping to block or falling back to cover the dump ball. Finally, the mental demands of the game in tight situations make it important that players learn to deal with pressure so that errors are not made.

In a quality performance I need to be aware of all these demands so that I can prepare and practise hard in my training sessions.

Examiners' feedback

This is a clear and detailed response. The candidate gives a good descriptive account and demonstrates sound logical and analytical thinking.

4/4

Qualities required for top performance

> **Key concept 2**
> Technical, physical, personal and special qualities of performance.

The knowledge you will acquire from studying this **key concept** will help you to understand about the qualities considered important to ensure a quality performance.

1. Technical qualities
2. Physical qualities
3. Personal qualities
4. Special qualities

These qualities are needed when:

- responding to the specific challenges of activities
- selecting and applying skills
- processing information.

Depending on the performance situation, you may use these to a greater or lesser degree. Applied correctly they can be the only or main determiner of the outcome (winning or losing).

What makes a quality performance?

Looking at the pictures of these elite performers should already incite your opinion of a quality performance! Refer back to these as we discuss each quality in turn.

A quality performance requires:

- a wide repertoire of skills
- control and fluency in the application and execution of skills
- an ability to make appropriate decisions in challenging situations
- a controlled mental state.

Technical qualities

To be successful in sport it is essential to demonstrate the technical qualities associated with the activity. This requires the performer to:

- assess the immediate performance challenge with split second timing
- appropriately select and apply the relevant technique to deal with the challenge
- execute the selected technique with precision, control, timing, accuracy and fluency.

Importantly, this may require precision of whole body application; most certainly dexterity of both sides of the body – right and left side management.

During performance the reliance on these technical qualities is high, as the interaction between movement, skill selection and application are played consecutively, for example, think about the tennis player who has to engage in baseline rallies.

The benefits of possessing technical qualities are:

- makes performance purposeful
- reduces unforced errors
- promotes error detection.

Note: you will study this information in more depth if you are examining some or more of the following: Skills and Technique, **key concepts** 2 and 3; Structures, Strategies and Composition, **key concept** 2.

Top Tip

If you have understood about technical qualities, then you will be able to think of the technical qualities *you* display when applying skills to meet strategies or compositional elements of your sport.

Physical qualities

Undoubtedly performers need to possess physical qualities associated with the activity/tasks/skills/techniques and application of structure, strategy or compositional element.

This requires the performer to:

- apply skills effectively for the duration of the specific activity/event
- maintain work-rate effectively for the duration of the specific activity/event
- fulfil role-related responsibilities effectively for the duration of the specific activity/event.

Importantly, this may require one or both of:

- whole body actions with bursts of energy for immediate or sustained periods of time
- isolated body parts with bursts of energy for immediate or sustained periods of time.

During performance the reliance on producing fitness will depend on the activity and task to be performed. Consider this statement from Jim Loehr:

'Competing in an event – physically, mentally, emotionally – requires energy. When the energy is gone the fight is all but over.'

The benefits of possessing appropriate **physical** qualities are:

- effectiveness of skill or role
- enables the performer to perform to their potential
- work-rate maintained for the duration of the game/event/meet/routine
- greater energy release to deal with mental and emotional stress.

Note: you will study this information in more depth if you are examining some or more of the following: Preparation of the Body, **key concepts** 2, 3 and 5; Structures, Strategies and Composition **key concept** 1.

Personal qualities

Singularly, the personal qualities that a performer possesses can be the difference between winning and losing – being effective or ineffective in performances.

Personal qualities reflect personal traits or characteristics such as self discipline, motivation/determination and an ability to handle emotional pressure.

This requires the performer to:

- maintain composure to apply skills effectively
- maintain work rate effectively
- fulfil role-related responsibilities effectively
- remain positive, determined and motivated

  often in front of crowds

  dealing with expectations

  dealing with failure

  dealing with frustration/cheating.

Importantly, this will require:

- total focus, concentration and determination on the immediate task; as an individual as part of a team
- an ability to block out factors affecting performance – both internal/external.

During performance, the personal qualities (traits) displayed are very much linked to inherent/genetic factors. Competent performers will use this potential to their benefit.

The benefits of possessing personal qualities are

- control of emotions
- managing anxiety/stress
- performing to potential
- having that never-say-die approach
- meeting challenges.

Note: you will study this information in more depth if you are examining some or more of the following: Performance Appreciation, **key concept** 4, Skills and Techniques, **key concepts** 1 and 3, Preparation of the Body, **key concept** 3.

Special qualities

The special qualities that a performer possess is what makes them stand out and relates to their unique trademark, the ability to do that little bit of magic.

This requires the performer to:

- have a wide repertoire of skills and abilities
- recognise opportunity within the performance challenge and execute the skill at the correct time.

Importantly, this will be evident in the ability to:

- fake intent, disguise or improvise intention
- be creative and produce opportunity
- inspire others, motivate and excite the spectators

- apply skills with maximum ease, control and flair
- consistently create an element of surprise.

During performance the special qualities displayed are very much linked to inherent unique ability. Competent performers will select and apply skills at will.

The benefits of possessing special qualities are:

- the performer is exciting and spectacular to watch
- gains in controlling play with the creation of space, time and options.

Note: you will study this information in more depth if you are examining some or more of the following: Performance Appreciation, **key concept** 4; Skills and Techniques, **key concepts** 1 and 3.

A point to consider

'The content of your character is your choice. Day by day, what you choose, what you think and what you do is who you become ...'

Anon

Quick Task

In relation to your own performance, write up the technical, physical, personal and special qualities you feel you possess. Give a detailed account of how the qualities you display differ from that of a model performer. Keep this as part of your study notes. It will help you to recall information more efficiently.

Summary

Technical, physical, personal and special qualities

Why has it been important to learn about this **key concept**?

Learning about this **key concept** has a range of benefits:

1. You will be more knowledgeable about how to evaluate strengths and weaknesses of performance.
2. You will be able to link this understanding to make sense of other **key concepts** as you study the other **analysis areas**.
3. You will broaden your appreciation of performance development from a sports science perspective.

For example, you will be able to consider:

- the importance of data/information gathering methods to highlight qualities displayed in isolation/during performance/future performances
- the analysis of data/information gathered to compare to model performers
- which training/practice methods would produce quickest results to improve all-round efficiency
- the influences on mental alertness and emotional stability
- different stages of learning
- the importance of feedback, motivation and concentration.

Top Tip

Remember these are just a few examples. If you have understood this **key concept** then you will be able to offer more examples from your own experiences.

Using these strategies in the exam

Remember, in your exam you may be asked to demonstrate your understanding of this **key concept** by *recalling* the information.

In this instance, you could be asked:

- describe the qualities or select at least two from four of the qualities that you display
- describe the qualities you would expect to see in a quality performance
- a quality performance looks effortless; with reference to specific qualities explain the qualities likely to be evident.

Alternatively you could be asked to demonstrate how you were able to make use of this acquired knowledge. For example, you could be asked to:

- explain why your performances may differ from that of a model performer
- describe a weakness you have in relation to at least one quality and explain the effect this had on your performance
- discuss the training programme you designed to address the weakest quality evident in your performance.

Exam Success

Look back at the commands words on page 9.

Quick Task

Discuss how in practice situations the qualities you possess are often displayed consistently and effectively – yet in competitive situations you can sometimes underperform.

Keep this as part of your study notes. It will help you to recall information more efficiently.

Improving your exam technique

Let us examine a past paper question and response.

Good exam technique

1. READ the question.
2. NOTE the mark value.
3. CONSIDER the **command word** (this has been embolden for you).
4. REFLECT on what the **command word** is telling you to do.

Sample question, answer and feedback

Question

'Quality performance requires a balance of technical, physical, personal and special qualities.'

In an activity of your choice, **describe** three different performance qualities that are evident in your current performance.   6 marks

Now read the sample answer

Note: the description word/phrase has been highlighted in blue.

I play central defender for my school football team. I feel that I possess a range of different technical, physical and personal qualities, which helps me to play effectively. Technically I am quite gifted; I have a wide repertoire of skills and can consistently control the ball with my head, chest and feet. I am able to deliver my passes accurately from a range of distances and accurately judge the pace of the ball. Obviously my best quality is in my ability to body challenge, protect the ball and tackle without giving away too many fouls. I feel that in this department I look in total control.

I feel I have high levels of physical fitness, particularly strength, with an ability to hold off strong challenges from my opponents, both on the ground and in the air. I have good speed endurance, which lets me move up to attack when needed and back quickly to defend on a counter attack. I am fairly quick and can jostle to deny space to limit the opposition's attack. The pace and tempo changes rapidly, I feel that I have the required level of cardio-respiratory endurance to let me compete for every ball possible.

I am a very competitive person and never give up, even if we find ourselves behind in a match. I feel I lead by example, I do not often lose my temper and I am really motivated to win. I feel this personal determination inspires my teammates to do well. I find it easy to concentrate and always remain focussed on the ball, space, positioning of my opponents and teammates as this helps me to make the right decisions during the game. I am also fearless when it comes to tackling.

Examiners' feedback

This is a clear and detailed response. The writer gives a good descriptive account and demonstrates sound logical and analytical thinking. Note the three discrete paragraphs with each section gaining two marks.   6/6

Mental influences on performance

> **Key concept 3**
> Making sense of the mental factors influencing performance.

The knowledge you will acquire from studying this **key concept** will help you understand about the various mental factors that will influence performance.

You will also reflect on the methods commonly used to deal with controlling mental state. This will broaden your appreciation of 'mental toughness' and challenge your thinking.

Mental state

Taking part in sport is demanding and is a continuous interplay between *technical ability, fitness* and most importantly about *emotions, perception* and *judgement*. Mental state refers to the ability to deal with stress and manage emotions. A person's mental state can greatly affect behaviour and performance. Firstly, consider the difference between stress and emotions.

- Stress is the energy you use thinking and concentrating.
- Emotions are the energy you use feeling, fear, failure, anger etc.

For example, when swimming in a race, *mental stress* is thinking about the tactics to be applied and *emotional stress* is worrying about the outcome.

Depending on your individual *personality* traits/characteristics will determine how you will handle your *mental state* – before/during/after performance. Personality refers to your psychological make-up, for example temperament, intelligence, beliefs, attitudes, values and interests. The development of personality is partly due to inherited characteristics (nature) and partly due to experiences and upbringing (nurture).

According to the psychologist Eysenck, two *dimensions* of personality exist. Extrovert and Introvert. Extroverts enjoy stress; they relish competitive challenges and immediately respond to stimuli. Introverts on the other hand, respond to challenges more slowly and can allow stress level to affect their performance.

Personality characteristics

The diagram offers *some* examples of what we mean by personality traits/characteristics. You may recognise your own personality traits from this. Within a sporting context, research has proven 'extroverts' are the most successful.

Analysis Area 1 Performance Appreciation

Your skill learning and ability to apply skills effectively is very much linked to mental factors. The potential you achieve is strengthened with a positive state of mind. Often excellence and success during performance is a result of increased self-confidence and ability to focus on the task rather than worry about the outcome.

The important thing here is to recognise that performers at all levels have difficulty staying cool under pressure. The problem with anger is that it usually disturbs focus, disrupts intensity levels, and upsets rhythm and clear thinking all at once. Competitive performance is very frustrating at times but it is even harder to master with anger. The performer who learns to modify and control anger often controls the outcome too.

Recognising these different personality traits makes sense of *why* mental state can have either a positive or negative affect on performance.

The main factors that influence mental state are:

- level of arousal – the state of readiness, i.e. being positive or negative
- anxiety, two main types – cognitive and somatic.

Anxiety

Cognitive anxiety refers to the inner feelings/thoughts. For example, 'I am feeling really confident about the match today ... I am worried about playing because ...'

This is linked to:

- importance of competition/event
- self confidence/frustration/fear of failure
- expectations of self/coach/parents/spectators.

Somatic anxiety refers to the physiological response that takes place and how your body reacts. For example, increased heart rate, sweaty palms, butterflies in the stomach, concentration lapse etc.

When feelings shift from confidence to fear, powerful changes occur in the brain's chemistry.

This is linked to changes in the blood stream as a result of the effects of adrenalin release (blood sugars that are stored in the muscles known as glycogen). This 'fight or flight' heightens the body's capacity to respond and critically affects co-ordination, balance, concentration and muscle response.

Controlling somatic anxiety during performance can be quite difficult and is reliant on experience/self confidence/internal feedback. It is crucial however to learn how to manage this type of anxiety as often the aggression displayed or unforced errors that appear can hinder the effectiveness of the performance.

Note: you will study this information in more depth if you are examining some or more of the following: Performance Appreciation, **key concept** 4; Preparation of the Body, **key concept** 3; Skills and Techniques, **key concept** 1.

This is where your studies in biology will help.

Methods of conquering anxiety

Application of the following techniques as part of your training will improve your ability to deal with anxiety.

- Visualisation – this involves you imagining how it would feel to ....
- Imagery/mental rehearsal – this involves going over in your mind precise sequence/movement patterns as sometimes a set routine helps.
- Deep breathing – involves controlled attempt to relax and slow breathing rate to regain focus/composure.
- Self talk – involves repeating key words or phrases to motivate regain focus/composure.
- Progressive relaxation – involves systematically tensing and relaxing specific muscle groups.

These techniques help 'train the brain'. By purposely slowing down brain activity you develop greater control of concentration and arousal; this will be characterised by feeling more confident/relaxed.

Remember, under pressure you will always crack at your weakest point – be it, technical, physical, tactical or mental – therefore in training practise harder at your weaknesses.

The secret here is to do what works best for you. And remember it is not just in a sporting context that you may feel anxiety (for example, preparing for your exams). The last chapter of this book gives advice on how to deal with this (pages 107 & 108).

Summary

Mental factors

Why has it been important to learn about this **key concept**?

Learning about this **key concept** has a range of benefits:

1. You will be more knowledgeable about how to evaluate strengths and weaknesses of performance.
2. You will be able to link this understanding to make sense of other **key concepts** as you study the other **analysis areas**.
3. You will broaden your appreciation of performance development from a sports science perspective.

For example, you will be able to consider:

- the different types of anxiety and reference this against how you deal with pressure
- the most relevant practice methods to enhance these qualities in your own performance
- how model/elite performers offer good/poor examples of dealing with pressure
- how the media reports performance values.

Top Tip

Remember these are just a few examples. If you have understood this **key concept** then you will be able to offer more examples from your own experiences.

  This is where your studies in English and Modern studies will help.

Using these strategies in the exam

Remember, in your exam you may be asked to demonstrate your understanding of this Key concept by *recalling* the information.

In this instance, you could be asked to:

- describe the mental factors that can affect performance
- describe a situation where negative and or positive thoughts affected your performance
- explain what you understand about controlling emotions/managing anxiety.

Alternatively you could be asked to demonstrate how you were able to make use of this acquired knowledge. For example, you could be asked to:

- explain why your control of mental strength may differ from that of a model performer
- discuss how your performance can be affected more in competition than in practice
- explain in detail the measures you took to develop your ability to be more mentally prepared for performances.

Exam Success

Look back at the commands words on page 9.

Quick Task

Write up how effectively you focus and remain calm when performing.

Would others agree with your opinion? Discuss.

Keep this as part of your study notes and revise regularly. This will help you to recall information more efficiently.

Improving your exam technique

Let us examine a past paper question and response.

This time you are looking at a discussion of related facts for 6 marks. Firstly, to help you make sense of how the examiner is testing mental factor understanding, you have the opportunity to read part a) of the same question before considering the response to part b) of the question.

Good exam technique

1. READ the question.
2. NOTE the mark value.
3. CONSIDER the **command word** (this has been embolden for you).
4. REFLECT on what the **command word** is telling you to do.

Sample question, answer and feedback

Question

Choose an activity. Select a mental factor that had a negative effect on your performance. What method(s) did you use to overcome this difficulty? Why was the method(s) appropriate?   6 marks

Now read the sample answer

Note: the description word/phrase has been highlighted in blue. When an explanation has been offered, this has been highlighted in green.

Top Tip

Practise giving this amount of detail in your answers and you are well on your way to a good pass.

During the course of any game players will make mistakes, as a central defender it crucial that I read play and be aware of the positioning of my opponents. A poor pass back to my goalkeeper almost caused a goal. Instead of forgetting about it I let it get to me. I hate letting my teammates down and worried more about what they might say rather than refocus and make sure I was concentrating. I started to get panicky and have negative thoughts. In 1v1 challenges I tried to compensate and went in too heavy; I was in danger of being carded. Losing control of my emotions upset my decision-making and I started to make more unforced errors. This was early in the game and I knew I had to do something about it if I were to help my teammates and stay on the park. When the ball was up-field I used 'self talk' and repeated in my head buzz words to keep me calmer and more focused on my job. It also helped to get shouted at by my teammates, I responded positively to their criticisms and took a few seconds to regroup and think before tackling. I found this improved my judgment, which in turn raised my confidence. At half time, our team talk helped and gave me the time to channel my energies to more positive thinking. Self talk, is appropriate as it only takes seconds to complete and helps self determination. Another good thing about 'self talk' is that it can happen simultaneously to the decisions I make, for example as I decide to slide tackle I can talk to myself at the same time to give me that edge. As I close down on the opposition forward I can hear myself say 'mine' or 'Ian's' as I slide my foot in to push the ball clear. Using these buzz words kept me more focused and improved the consistency in my play.

Examiners' feedback

This is a clear and detailed response. The writer offers good personal examples throughout the answer of how loss of control affected performance. The method for dealing with this difficulty was relevant and appropriate. The writer exhibits good analytical thinking.   6/6

Model performers

> **Key concept 4**
> Use of appropriate model performers.

The knowledge you will acquire from studying this **key concept** will help you understand about the benefits of considering model performers. Model performers exist at all ability levels and are used in the main as the widest form of feedback. This feedback can be offered in a variety of ways, for example, visual or verbal with the intent to improve the learning and development of skilled abilities and application of practice or training.

The Olympic Games and the study of model performers

Think of the impact of the 2008 Olympic Games. Many of these athletes when interviewed agreed that when younger they had been inspired by model performers to give of their best and maximise their potential. All of them were committed to representing their country to gain the highest achievement possible.

Whilst not all of you can aspire to Olympic achievements, the study of model performers will improve your skill learning and development in a number of ways by:

* providing various types of feedback, both visual and verbal, that can be qualitative, quantitive, diagnostic in nature
* identifying performance strengths and weaknesses
* increasing confidence, motivation
* providing challenge in practice/training/competition
* inspiring higher levels of achievement
* encouraging comparative analysis
* inspiring to copy ideas/techniques and/or application to strategy or composition
* design/planning practice/targets/training
* providing exemplification of good sportsmanship and conduct.

A good starting point is to compare your performance to that of a model performer. Using various methods of analysis, this will give you a bench mark against which you can set targets as you work towards improving your own performance.

Using model performers as inspiration

Remember model performers can help you improve ALL aspects of your performance – *fitness, skill, mental control, application of strategy/composition*.

Regardless of how you decide to use them, the importance will be linked to your understanding of the need to:

- identify your performance strengths and weaknesses
- collect reliable information to evaluate progress through various data methods
- ensure realistic targets are set and met during/after training – *monitoring and review*
- practise/train using relevant methods.

To make best use of model performers you need to be motivated to learn/copy/mimic. You need to concentrate on what advice is being given and act upon it.

Model performers can excel at any performance level:

- in your class
- club level
- international level.

In summary, they are talented, highly skilled, physically fit and mentally tough in order to efficiently sustain the required energy demands and challenges of the activity

Note: you will study this information in more depth if you are examining some or more of the following: Performance Appreciation, **key concepts** 2 and 3; Preparation of the Body, **key concepts** 3; Skills and Techniques, **key concepts** 1, 2 and 3; Structure, Strategies and Composition, **key concepts** 2.

Think about your other subjects for example, art, drama, music, technical education. Can you think of students in these classes whom you would consider model performers? If so did this help you to improve upon your own performance?

Remember there is nothing more infectious than leading by example.

A point to consider

'People who are unable to motivate themselves must be content with mediocrity, no matter how impressive their other talents.'

Andrew Carnegie

Summary

Model performers

Why has it been important to learn about this **key concept**?

Learning about this **key concept** has a range of benefits:

1. You will be more knowledgeable about how to evaluate personal strengths and weaknesses/make comparisons.
2. You will be able to link this understanding to make sense of other **key concepts** as you study the other analysis areas.
3. You will have broadened your appreciation of performance development from a sports science perspective. Thus equipping you to debate and substantiate your opinion.

For example, you will be able to offer opinion, equipping you with the skills to debate and substantiate your opinion about:

- the use of different data methods to make comparative analysis
- the importance of feedback, concentration, motivation
- the various levels/qualities that elite and model performers display.

Top Tip

Remember these are just a few examples. If you have understood this **key concept** then you will be able to offer more examples from your own experiences.

Using these strategies in the exam

Remember, in your exam you may be asked to demonstrate your understanding of this **key concept** by *recalling* the information.

In this instance you could be asked to:

- describe how you used model performers to help identify your performance strengths and weaknesses
- describe what qualities you would expect to see in a model performer
- describe the impact a model performer has in the development of a) skill, b) fitness, c) strategy or composition.

Alternatively you could be asked to demonstrate how you were able to make use of this acquired knowledge. For example, you could be asked to:

- discuss the benefits of studying model performances
- explain why your performances may differ from that of a model performer
- discuss how you used a model performer to reach your short or longer term goals.

Exam Success

Look back at the commands words on page 9.

> These types of questions are designed to increase your confidence to state your opinion. This happens significantly when studying English.

Quick Task

Write up how you have used model performers to help you improve an aspect of your performance. What qualities would you expect to see in a model performance?

Keep this as part of your study notes and revise regularly. This will help you to recall information more efficiently.

Improving your exam technique

Let us examine a past paper question and response.

This time you are looking at a discussion of related facts for 4 marks. Firstly, to help you make sense of how the examiner is testing model performer understanding, you have the opportunity to *read* parts a) and b) of the same question before *answering* part c) of the question

Good exam technique

1. READ the question.
2. NOTE the mark value.
3. CONSIDER the **command word** (this has been embolden for you).
4. REFLECT on what the **command word** is telling you to do.

Sample question, answer and feedback

Question

a) Choose one activity. **Describe** what you regard as a model performer in this activity.   4 marks
b) **Compare** and **contrast** your performance to the model performance you have described in part a).   6 marks
c) **Discuss** the benefits that can be gained from using appropriate models of performance.   4 marks

Now read the sample answer

Note: when a discursive word/phrase has been offered this has been highlighted in yellow.

There are many benefits to be gained from watching model performers; importantly they can inspire me to achieve higher performance standards. By watching them I can get a visual picture of their effectiveness and get different ideas on how to execute moves, skills or tactics so that I could copy them for my own benefits. By watching model performers I could set my performance targets – I could try and copy what I saw and during practice work towards making my performance more effective for the longer term. Another benefit that could be gained from the model performer is that I could receive valuable feedback as they can identify my weaknesses and offer constructive criticism about the best way to develop my own skill level. They can be a source of motivation either by encouragement or aspiration. Model performers can also provide me with competitive challenge and either play against me or feed appropriately allowing me to practise. With an ability to play at half pace the model performer can accurately set up action allowing me to get the most from my training. Model performers can come from different sources either from someone in my class or team or district/national performer.

Top Tip

Practise giving this amount of detail in your answers and you are well on your way to a good pass.

Examiners' feedback

This is a clear and detailed response. The writer offers good examples of how model performers would benefit performance and links knowledge to target setting. The writer exhibits good critical thinking.

4/4

Planning your training

> **Key concept 5**
> Planning and managing personal performance improvement.

The knowledge you will acquire from studying this **key concept** will help you to understand about planning effective training.

Developing a specific programme

Ensuring that training is effective demands careful planning. All performers have different needs relative to the activity they are involved in. Therefore, the most important planning consideration is that it must be specific. This means the programme has to be developed to meet the individual needs of the performer, taking into account gender, age, strengths, weaknesses, activity demands, objectives, training facilities etc. The planning considerations of any programme are to:

- gather details about the individual – strengths, weaknesses, role played, performance demand
- identify the fitness types to develop – physical, technical, mental, skill-related, tactical – appropriate to the activity
- identify appropriate tests to monitor fitness and performance status
- design, apply and adjust the programme
- monitor and review progress.

Performance analysis

What is performance analysis, and how can it be integrated within and benefit performance?

An essential factor of managing training is testing, measuring and recording. This promotes performance analysis.

Many sports are complex to commit to record due to the continuous, dynamic and fast action, especially team games, gymnastics and dance. It is difficult, if not impossible, to observe and remember all the key events occurring within a training session, match, meet or event. Yet analysis based on accurate *observation* and *recall* is a key tool for improving performance.

Depending on the training objectives, i.e. the agreed goals, initial performance status and subsequent performance evaluations ensure peak performance is reached. To do this successfully depends on your ability to assemble information, sort it, evaluate it and draw conclusions from it.

Valid and reliable testing procedures and recording methods are available for this purpose, and the meanings of *valid* and *reliable* in relation to a test, measurement or recording method are as follows:

- A *valid* method is defined as being appropriate, meaningful, logical, justifiable to use, backing opinion to support claims for improved performance, and the data is obtained accurately. To make claims more valid, more than one method should be used or used repeatedly to compare to national norms – this avoids human error or bias *(subjectivity)*.

- A *reliable* method is suitable for purpose, used in a consistent manner and/or can be easily replicated. For example, a reliable test for measuring flexibility is the 'sit and reach' test. The test results can then be compared against national norms and/or an observation checklist can be compared against performance criteria (see page 76–77 for more detailed information).

WHY TEST? The results can be used to:	THE TESTING PROCESS The whole measurement/ evaluation process involves:	RECORDING METHODS These methods can be used in and out of activity ensuring validity/reliability issues.	PURPOSE		
			Qualitative	Quantitative	Diagnostic
Indicate strengths and weaknesses	The selection of characteristics to be measured	Standardised fitness tests – record sheets		*	
Support monitoring and review		Scattergram – diagram of ...		*	
	The selection of a suitable method of measuring	Observation checklists – qualitative data	*		*
Measure improvement	The collection of that data/ information	Match analysis sheets – quantifiable data		*	
Predict future performance		Player profile – record sheets/ checklists	*		*
Motivate the performer to attain goals	The analysis of the collected data/ information	Questionnaires – record sheets	*	*	
		Flowcharts – graphs/notation sheets	*		*
	The selection and application of an appropriate training programme	Record times – personal best sheets		*	
		Video tape, digital photography, computer programmes	*	*	*
		Dictaphone – verbal commentary	*	*	*

Planning and goal-setting

Planning training will only have the desired effect if a systematic approach to identify the work to be carried out will achieve agreed objectives or *goals*.

These goals are linked and defined as short- and long-term and ensure optimal performance is reached at the correct time.

Once these goals are agreed the performer must be knowledgeable and select from the various methods of *training* and *practice* the most relevant to produce the quickest effect.

Essentially the training demands must simulate the activity demands if the performer is to improve efficiently.

The performer must therefore be aware of *how to train*. Basically the choices are to train in the activity (often referred to as a *conditioning* approach), out of the activity or a combination of both. Most importantly the principles of training or effective practice must be applied to ensure improvement.

Analysis Area 1 Performance Appreciation

TRAINING IN THE ACTIVITY	TRAINING OUT OF THE ACTIVITY	COMBINATION OF BOTH
Can address • Technical weaknesses via range of progressive practices • Physical weaknesses via repetition/duration periods • Mental weaknesses via rehearsal/imagery/breathing techniques • Tactical weaknesses via range of pressure drills/set pieces/routines	Can address • Physical weaknesses via circuit, weight, cross training, interval, fartlek, continuous, plyometric training • Mental weaknesses via related breathing, imagery techniques applied during training/practices	Can address • Short-term and long term goals-paced • Phases of training- planned • Emphasis on fitness-overload/progression
The benefits • ALL of the above can be interlinked therefore saves time • Can be more motivating/fun/varied • Enables individual/group or team work • Provides competition/challenge • Principles of training/practice can easily be applied • Training focus can be prioritised and varied • Can be fitted around other commitments	The benefits • Some of the above can be interlinked • Can motivate to attain personal goals • Enables the use of specialised equipment • Can be fitted around other commitments • Facilitates extra personal gain specific to individual role/performance demands • Principles of training/practice can easily be applied	The benefits • Offers variety • Enables performer to manage training when injury/other commitments clash • Facilitates extra personal gain • Principles of training/practice can easily be applied

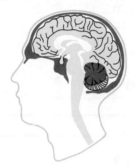 

The most important part of managing your programme is to ensure progression. If the training objective is *fitness* based then the principles of training should be applied; if the training objective is *skill/tactical/mental* based then the principles of effective practice should be applied.

PRINCIPLES OF TRAINING	PRINCIPLES OF EFFECTIVE PRACTICE
Overloading is the most important principle of fitness training. Simply put, it is basically an increase in demand to force bodily adaptation. Altering the following factors will increase in fitness level or athletic performance.	SMART or SMARTER
	S – goals must be specific
Using the following acronym may help you to remember	M – training targets should be measurable
FITT:	A – goals should be adjustable
F – Frequency that refers to how often you exercise	R – goals must be realistic
I – Intensity that refers to how hard you exercise	T – training targets should be time-based
T – Time that refers to how long you exercise for	E – goals should be exciting and challenging
T – Type that refers to the kind of exercise you undertake	R – goals should be recorded

Note: increasing your understanding of these principles will develop your appreciation of when to apply them to ensure the programme you design and use will be effective. You will also cover these principles when studying the **analysis areas** Preparation of the Body, **key concept** 4, and Skills and techniques, **key concept** 3.

Monitoring and reviewing progress

The final stage of managing training is to monitor and review progress – this lets us know whether or not our training has been effective. The meanings of monitor and review are as follows:

- monitor relates to an *ongoing* process, i.e. when you want to analyse/check/observe your performance status
- review relates to the end process, i.e. when you want to evaluate/re-examine/assess your performance status.

To ensure these processes are valid it is important to use the same test, measurement or recording method as before. This ensures effective comparative analysis to take place and prioritises areas for future development (see table on previous page).

Why monitor and review performance?

What is the purpose of these processes? The answer – primarily for feedback.

This feedback essentially:

- defines strengths and weaknesses
- informs future planning and training.

There are two main types of feedback:

1. Intrinsic (*internal* – what you know and feel yourself).
2. Extrinsic (*external* – information gained from other sources – verbal, visual, written, kinaesthetic, vestibular).

You will learn to offer and receive feedback that is:

- qualititive – statements that reflect the quality of control, precise, effort, flair, creativity etc.
- quantitive – data that supports consistency and accuracy, often statistical
- diagnostic – statements that reflect error detection and/or cause and effect.

Learning how to make best use of feedback will:

- enable you interpret and analyse results
- offer comparative analysis
- justify improvements in your performance
- plan for future development needs.

Feedback must be integrated within training to ensure progression.

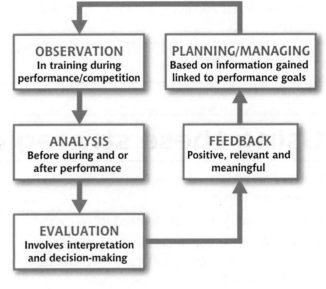

OBSERVATION
In training during
performance/competition

PLANNING/MANAGING
Based on information gained
linked to performance goals

ANALYSIS
Before during and or
after performance

FEEDBACK
Positive, relevant and
meaningful

EVALUATION
Involves interpretation
and decision-making

A point to consider

'You need to be aware of what others are doing, applaud their efforts, acknowledge their successes, and encourage them in their pursuits. When we all help one another, everybody wins.'

Jim Stovall

Summary

Planning and managing personal performance improvement

Why has it been important to learn about this key concept?

Learning about this **key concept** has a range of benefits:

1. You will be more knowledgeable about how to evaluate training requirements to match specific individual or activity demands.
2. You will be able to link this understanding to make sense of other **key concepts** as you study the other **analysis areas**.
3. You will broaden your appreciation of performance development from a sports science perspective.

For example, you will be able consider:

- the purpose of planning and managing training
- the purpose of testing, measuring, recording performance
- how to select and apply different types of training, practise to match specific performance.
- the application of training principles and principles of effective practice to ensure improvement.

Top Tip

Remember these are just a few examples. If you have understood this **key concept** then you will be able to offer more examples from your own experiences.

Using these strategies in the exam

Remember, in your exam you may be asked to demonstrate your understanding of this **key concept** by *recalling* the information.

In this instance you could be asked to:

- describe what you understand by planning
- discuss – short-term and long-term planning is crucial for performance improvement
- training can be organised in the activity, out the activity or both
- explain the advantages of at least two methods.

Alternatively you could be asked to demonstrate how you were able to make use of this acquired knowledge. For example, you could be asked to:

- explain why your performances may differ from that of a model performer
- describe a programme of work you have used to benefit your performance
- explain the principles you applied to ensure your programme was effective
- discuss the improvements you made to your performance as a result of your training – which methods of evaluation did you use?

Exam Success

Look back at the commands words on page 9.

 > In many sciences, social sciences and also in maths you will often be required to calculate effects of improved performances or queries. Use this knowledge to support your understanding.

Quick Task

Outline any planning considerations you require to make for your performance development in an activity. Explain how you would prioritise areas requiring development.

Keep this as part of your study notes. It will help you to recall information more efficiently.

Improving your exam technique

Let us examine a past paper question and response.

Firstly, to help you make sense of how the examiner is testing your understanding of training considerations, you have the opportunity to examine parts a) and b) of the same question.

This time you are looking at a discussion of the consideration of training for 6 marks and then how to monitor effectiveness for 4 marks.

Good exam technique

1. READ the question.
2. NOTE the mark value.
3. CONSIDER the **command word** (this has been embolden for you).
4. REFLECT on what the **command word** is telling you to do.

Sample question, answer and feedback

Question

a) **Discuss** the importance of long- and short-term goals. Give examples of the goals you set to improve your performance.   6 marks
b) How did you monitor your performance as you worked towards achieving your goals?   4 marks

Read the sample answer to part a

Note: when an explanation has been offered this has been highlighted in green. Discursive points are highlighted in yellow.

Importantly taking account of short term goals will enable me to work effectively to achieve my long term goals.

Planning is crucial as I needed to think about what I wanted to achieve immediately, for example, maintaining my general fitness and consistency of my technical abilities and importantly stay injury free. This would have an impact on my training priorities for my long term goals to help our team win the league for a third consecutive year. This makes tremendous demands on me as an individual but the same demands are there for us as a team unit. The season is physically and mentally demanding therefore our preparation to achieve goals is crucial. As I have said our short term goals were to maintain general fitness, refine our technical abilities and win our weekly league matches. Our longer term goals were to develop more specific aspects of fitness and improve our tactical plans so that we would have more practised alternatives when playing against our rivals.

For example, short term goals were addressed by weekly training schedules; three times of 1 to 1 + 1/2 hours. In these sessions we worked on our fitness and skill maintenance by using a conditioning approach.

Specific drills were used in the form of a six station circuit aimed at improving role related duties of passing, tackling, kicking and line out throwing etc. These sessions finished off with the use of tackle bags in a 1v1 or 2v1 drives to help improve our defensive skills, this kept us motivated as it was game like and more challenging; mini games were also incorporated.

In the longer term, we planned to devote more time to our strategic play.

The league championships are usually a four team race. We have won the last two years but feel to ensure victory we need to improve our game plan and devise new tactics to give us the upper hand.

We had to be dedicated to team practice and work hard on both our fitness and skills and used repetitive practice of set plays to ensure application became automatic. At this time we relied heavily on video replay of previous performances to improve our tactics. We also reviewed the performances of our rivals so we could be ready when they presented us with challenges.

During this period our coach would experiment with players playing different roles so that we were all match fit and able to fulfil and or change roles at any time in the game, for example if we used substitutes. The incentive to win three in a row was the biggest goal we needed.

Examiners' feedback

Part a) This is a clear and detailed response. The writer clearly understands the importance of goal setting when planning training. There is sound evidence of critical thinking as the writer offers good examples to support points made throughout the discussion.

6/6

Now read sample answer to part b

Look at the response offered. Just to remind you in this question you are being asked to describe.

Note: when a description has been offered this has been highlighted in green.

b) To be honest monitoring was easy as it is a very important part to of our preparation throughout the season.

During training our progress is monitored in various ways. For our short-term goals, we used progress charts and record sheets of statistics of passing, line out successes etc. We then compared previous results, which gave us an incentive, i.e. we had to try and beat previous targets. During this period standard fitness tests were used to test specific areas related to cardio-respiratory, muscular endurance as well as speed and agility. Our coach would give us feedback and if required make us do extra training. The most reliable method of all was watching our league positioning, which appeared in the local newspaper.

In the longer term we focused on our target of championship succession. Video replay was the most reliable and powerful tool. With our coach we would sit together and pinpoint weaknesses take this back onto the training field and rehearse improved moves. Training as well as match play was recorded, with game statistics a very prominent feature of our discussion. Honesty being the best policy, we gave each other criticism when it was due. We knew each other well to accept it and used our own internal feedback to accept or reject points made. This proved to be right and as a result we tried even harder in practice the next week. The final way in which we monitored our progress was our parents who attended just about every game. They certainly told it like it was.

Top Tip

Practise giving this amount of detail in your answers and you are well on your way to a good pass.

Examiners' feedback

Part b) A clear and detailed description of how training was monitored is very apparent. The writer describes various tools of monitoring which are relevant.

4/4

How fit are you?

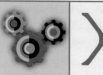

Key concept 1
Fitness assessment in relation to personal performance.

Remember in this **analysis area** you will be studying information that will help you to look at **specific** parts of your performance. In this **key concept** you will learn about related fitness needs specific to particular activities and also to role-related responsibilities. The focus will be on related activity and individual fitness types, demands fitness testing and planning training to improve your performance.

You will also learn about training approaches you can select in trying to improve your performance related fitness.

Fitness

Fitness is central to all activities. All performers have different fitness requirements relative to the *activity* they are involved in.

In order to plan improvements in your performance it is important to gather information on your initial level of fitness. To do this successfully depends on your ability to assemble information, sort it, evaluate it and draw conclusions from it.

When collecting information about your fitness it must be *specific* and *valid* in relation to:

- the demands of the activity, for example, physical/technical/mental/skill-related/tactical/compositional
- the individual fitness requirements to take part effectively, for example, the specific role you may play/perform.

The purpose of gathering information is it enables you to:

- find out which components of fitness are developed and which require further development
- find out your baseline/current level of fitness
- compare your results to national norms and/or others in your class/group
- plan a fitness programme for improvement
- set goals, both short-term and long-term
- remain motivated to attain goals set
- monitor your training and progress by comparing first results with later results *pre* and *post training*
- make informed judgements about the success and effectiveness of the training method(s) selected.

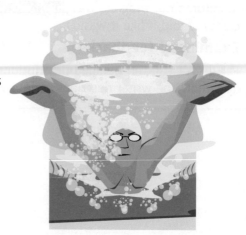

Your critical thinking will be evident dependent upon your selection of the most appropriate testing procedures and recording methods available for purpose. There are many to choose from and you will need to take into account validity and reliability issues.

Valid simply means what you are measuring is relevant/meaningful/logical or justifiable and backs up your claims or opinion.

For example, cardio-respiratory endurance (CRE) is important when swimming. Taking pulse counts to back up your claim for your CRE level would be considered a relevant and valid method to gather information for this aspect of fitness.

Reliable means used in a consistent manner, can be easily replicated and is suitable for the purpose.

For example, if you carried out the vertical jump test (Sargeant) for measuring explosive power, as the test procedures remain the same every time you do the test and national norms remain constant, the comparisons you offer are considered reliable.

You will have covered some of this in Performance Appreciation, **key concept** 5.

Methods

How do you decide which methods would be most appropriate?

Knowing that information can be gathered both *in the activity* and *outwith the activity* is a good starting point. Importantly, the methods you initially use should be used at the end of training to ensure your comparisons are more reliable.

Most test procedures are easy to carry out and should provide accurate and relevant information however issues relating to human error may feature as a problem.

Let us examine some of the methods you can use to test your fitness.

Fitness investigation outwith the activity

Here, standardised tests are used. These provide specific information about aspects of fitness, which can be compared to national norms and peers. Examples of these are as follows:

Physical fitness tests

- Harvard step test, 12 minute Cooper run, bleep test or multi-fitness test all for CRE.
- Sit and reach and trunk hyperextension for flexibility.
- Sit up test for muscular endurance.
- Hand grip/leg pull dynamometer for strength.
- 50-metre shuttle run for speed.
- Vertical/standing broad jump for power.

Skill-related fitness tests

- Illinois agility run for agility.
- One foot balance for balance.
- Ruler drop test for reaction time.
- Alternate hand throw and catch for co-ordination.

Mental fitness tests

- Questionnaires/self evaluation tests.
- Feedback both internal/external.

Using this information in the exam

In your exam you will be required to demonstrate critical thinking by selecting which test is the most appropriate to use for each aspect of fitness. In addition you must provide a detailed description of *how* the test is constructed and describe its *purpose*.

Here is a sample response:

The Vertical Jump or Sargeant Jump Test. Its purpose is to test explosive power.

When I used the Sargeant Jump Test I had to stand side on to a wall and reach up with my hand closest to the wall. Keeping my feet flat on the ground, the point of my fingertips was marked or recorded. This is called my standing reach. I had to stand away from the wall, and jump vertically as high as I could using both arms and legs to assist in projecting me upwards. I had to attempt to touch the wall at the highest point of my jump. The difference in distance between my standing reach height and my jump height was my score. The best of three attempts was recorded. I then compared my results to the national norms provided; this gave me my initial target to try and beat.

Fitness investigation in the activity

Fitness information can also be collected during your whole performance. This provides *objective* information, and the benefit of this is that it allows you to compare both fitness and whole performance competence.

Look at this relevant example from swimming. The *purpose* is to record a 320 metre time for an endurance swim.

Two-length blocks measured (40 metres)	Strokes	Pulse check	Time per two-lengths block
1/2	17	128	36.20
3/4	17	131	39.63
5/6	18	137	41.90
7/8	18	141	41.80
9/10	20	155	44.11
11/12	21	158	46.30
13/14	23	160	47.67
15/16	23	162	44.50

In the example above, the data provides the following types of information:

- length time
- stroke count
- pulse check
- personal best time.

Possible interpretations

This swimmer has poor local muscular endurance shown by increased time and number of strokes per length. Also each two-length time gets slower as the swim progresses. CRE is challenged, evident in heart rate variations via pulse check.

This information can now be used to plan an improvement programme that would hopefully lead to an improvement in local muscular endurance and CRE levels.

Training success will depend on planning, goal setting and applying training principles. On completion of training whole performance improvements should be evident in improved length and personal best times.

Another example of collecting information on your whole performance fitness within the activity is a time-related observation schedule. This is valid and very often used in conjunction with a video. This makes it easier to refer back to, take accurate statistics and makes interpretations and findings more *reliable*.

The example below relates to the specific aspect of fitness, CRE, and technical skills relative to role related responsibilities in rugby.

Activity = rugby, position = forward, 2 × 40 mins half															
WALKING				JOGGING				RUNNING				SPRINTING			
0–20	20–40	40–60	60–80	0–20	20–40	40–60	60–80	0–20	20–40	40–60	60–80	0–20	20–40	40–60	60–80
√√	√√	√√	√√	√√	√√	√√	√√	√√	√√	√√	√√	√√	√√	√√	√√
√	√√	√√	√√	√	√√	√√	√√	√√	√√	√√	√√	√√	√√	√	
		√	√√			√√	√√	√√	√√	√√	√	√√	√√		
			√√					√√	√√	√√		√√			

In the example above, the data provides the following types of information:

- discrete times within the game
- related technical skills within the game
- role within the game.

Possible interpretations

CRE level and performance level gets poorer as the game develops; evident from the comparison of sprinting and running in the later stages of the game compared to the first 40 minutes and the increase in the number of times the player walks and jogs compared to previously.

From this analysis the specific aspect of fitness required to be developed becomes evident.

- Scattergrams
- Video
- Match analysis sheets
- Record sheets
- Questionnaires, in particular for mental fitness where you could use tests that are computer-based, for example the SCAT test.

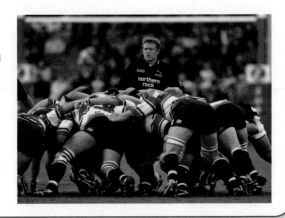

Regardless of the methods used it is most important that you *analyse and interpret* the data accurately. In relation to fitness evaluations, *interpreting* data usually involves calculations and percentages. Using this information allows you to identify your strengths and weaknesses and plan a programme for improvement.

When studying maths, geography and science for example, you are required to make calculations and interpret results.

Summary

Fitness assessment

Why has it been important to learn about this key concept?

Learning about this **key concept** has a range of benefits:

1. You will be more knowledgeable about how to assess fitness in terms of individual performance and activity specific demands.
2. You will be able to link this understanding to make sense of other **key concepts** as you study the other **analysis areas**.
3. You will understand the importance of fitness testing.
4. You will know what methods you could use to assess your fitness

For example, you will be able to consider:

- what tests are appropriate for particular aspects of fitness
- why test results must be accurate, valid and reliable
- what the purpose of a particular test is.

Using these strategies in the exam

Remember, in your exam you may be required to demonstrate your understanding of this **key concept** by recalling the information. In this instance, you could be asked to:

- describe the methods you used to assess your fitness in your chosen activity.

Alternatively you could be asked to demonstrate how you were able to make use of this acquired knowledge. For example, you could be asked to:

- explain why it is important to gather information on your level of fitness
- discuss the results from the information you gathered about your fitness.

Exam Success

Look back at the commands words on page 9.

Quick Task

List the methods you would use for the activities in your course. Think why they are valid and appropriate. Make sure you are able to describe them in detail and be able to explain what the results tell you about your performance.

Keep this as part of your study notes. It will help you to recall information more efficiently.

Improving your exam technique

Let us examine a past paper question and response.

This time you are looking for an explanation of how you gathered information on an aspect of fitness within an activity. Firstly, to help you make sense of how the examiner is testing your knowledge of the methods, it is important to *read* part (a) of the question – then *answer* part (b).

Good exam technique

1. READ the question.
2. NOTE the mark value.
3. CONSIDER the **command word** (this has been embolden for you).
4. REFLECT on what the **command word** is telling you to do.

Sample question, answer and feedback

Question

Choose an activity

a) **Describe** the physical, skill-related and mental fitness requirements for effective performance within your activity.

b) From the fitness requirements described in part a), select one aspect. **Explain** how you gathered information about it within the activity

Now read the sample answer

Note: the description word/phrase has been highlighted in blue and when an explanation has been offered this has been highlighted in green.

I have selected CRE, which is an aspect of physical fitness. To gather information about it I did the T5 swim test. This is a recognised test which you can do within the activity. The object was to swim front crawl for 5 minutes at an even pace. I was part of a group of four. Each person had a particular job to do – swimming, timing, counting or recording data. We changed each time one person had completed the swim until all of us had swam. The data was collected on a recording sheet. We recorded 20 metre split times and took stroke and breath counts. The total distance was recorded and divided by the time taken. An even pace confirmed that CRE was being tested. This gave me information on my level of CRE fitness and I was able to identify my strengths and weaknesses. From this information it allowed me to set targets for my training programme. I could also compare times to other classmates and give me an incentive during training to improve my overall time.

Examiners' feedback

This is a clear response with good description of method used with relevant explanations given as to how information was gathered in the activity.

The writer shows good acquired and applied knowledge.   4/4

Specific fitness needs and role responsibilities

> **Key concept 2**
> Application of different types of fitness in the development of activity-specific performance.

The focus will be on related activity and individual fitness types, demands fitness testing and planning training to improve your performance.

In this **key concept** you will learn about related fitness needs **specific** to particular activities and also to role-related responsibilities.

You will also learn about training approaches you can select in trying to improve your performance-related fitness.

Specific fitness needs

To perform effectively in an activity requires a wide range of technical, physical and mental skills. Each activity has different fitness requirements depending on the nature of the activity.

It is important that you become familiar with the *specific* fitness needs required for you to become effective in that activity.

For example in *football* all players require various physical, skill-related and mental aspects of fitness. These include stamina, speed endurance, strength, power, muscular endurance, balance, and managing emotions.

In *gymnastics* the performer requires various physical, skill-related and mental aspects of fitness. However here more emphasis is placed on strength, flexibility, agility, power, balance, coordination, motivation, determination and rehearsal.

Think about the activities you have done on your course. What activity-specific fitness needs do you require?

Specific role responsibilities

Fitness needs will often be determined by the *role* you play and the *responsibilities it entails*.

In basketball a centre requires particular fitness needs to be able to carry out the attacking and defensive duties. They must be able to get up and down the court quickly in the game so require a high level of cardio-respiratory endurance. They also need power in the legs to jump and compete for rebounds both offensively and defensively. They also need strength to hold off and block out opponents in rebounds and when defending.

However a guard in basketball will have different fitness needs. They require good agility so that when dribbling they can control the ball and change direction quickly to beat their defender and also to keep tight ball control. They need good speed to get past an opponent and be on the end of fast breaks.

These examples should reinforce your thinking when considering the different *specific* fitness needs of players/performers in a range of activities. This will influence your decisions when selecting the most appropriate training to develop your specific fitness needs.

Assessing your own needs

Before planning and selecting specific training in relation to the specific fitness needs or role-related needs, it is important to find out your own level of personal performance. This will be achieved by gathering information on your performance. This will allow you to gain information on your strength and weaknesses in relation to your fitness needs and to set specific objectives and training goals in order for you to try and improve your performance in the activity.

You will have covered the methods of gathering information on your fitness in more depth in Preparation of the Body, **key concept** 1 and goal setting in Performance Appreciation, **key concept** 5.

Once you have identified your fitness needs from the information gathered you must select the most relevant training approach to produce the desired effect of achieving the goals and objectives set.

Remember your training demands must simulate the activity specific requirements or role-related requirements if you are to improve your performance efficiently.

Quick Task

Choose two activities from your course. Compare and contrast the fitness needs for each activity. Would others agree with your opinion?

Keep this as part of your study notes. It will help you study to recall information more efficiently.

Approaches to training

You should be aware of what approach to use to improve your performance-related fitness. There are three approaches to consider:

- training within the activity (conditioning)
- training outwith the activity
- combination of both.

Training within the activity

This is where you are trying to develop your fitness by doing work in the activity. This can address all types of fitness and allows you to develop skill as well as fitness. Examples are shown below.

- Physical fitness in athletics for 800 metre running. I did Fartlek training, did eight laps – jogged the straights and ran the bends – without stopping, then did six short 60 metre sprints with a short 20 metre jog leading into each sprint – made demand similar to the end of an actual race.
- Skill-related fitness in hockey, working on particular set pieces like a penalty corner or working on particular drills involving skills such as dribbling, long passing and short passing.
- Mental fitness in football when playing short competitive games. I concentrated on controlling my emotions when things went wrong.

Methods of training you could use within the activity include:

- continuous training
- Fartlek
- interval training
- rehearsal imagery
- controlled breathing.

Training outwith the activity

This is where you are working on developing your fitness away from the activity using various methods to work on specific aspects of fitness.

For example:

To improve my cardio-respiratory endurance for my role as a midfielder in hockey, I carried out some circuit training in the games hall, doing high intensity work, work rest ratio 1:3, doing a series of exercises – step-ups, burpees, continuous running, three sets of exercises – working on each for 45 secs.

The methods of training you could use to train outwith the activity include:

- interval training
- continuous training
- circuit training
- weight training
- plyometrics
- imagery
- visualisation
- Fartlek.

Combination of both training in and outwith the activity

This is where you are developing fitness and/or skills within the activity and working on specific aspects of fitness that are important to the activity outwith it.

For example:

Swimming – I trained using a combination of training within activity and outwith activity. Within I used interval training, working on developing both anaerobic and aerobic fitness – did warm-up, then stroke improvement, a main set 6×50 metre swim with one minute recovery, a sub set 6×50 with 45 secs recovery, then warm down. Outwith the pool I did a weight training circuit, doing a series of exercises – three sets – and also some work on stepping machines and rowing machines to improve.

Methods of training used in a combination of both would be chosen from the methods listed in training within and outwith the activity.

Note: various methods of training can be used in each approach. You will have covered these in Preparation of the Body, **key concept** 4. Further information on approaches is also covered in Performance Appreciation **key concept** 5.

What are the benefits and advantages of each approach to training?

TRAINING IN THE ACTIVITY	TRAINING OUTWITH THE ACTIVITY	COMBINATION OF BOTH
• Can improve skills as well as working on fitness. • Can work on physical, skill related, mental and tactical weaknesses. • Can work on game-like routines and set pieces. • Can be challenging and motivating. • Allows variety in training. • Allows both individual and team work to improve. • Can simulate pressure demands of various situations similar in games.	• Can develop specific aspects of fitness. • Easy to set up training. • Uses specialised equipment. • Can be challenging and motivational. • Principles of training can be easily applied. • Can develop general fitness. • Can be adapted to suit fitness factors.	• Offers variety. • Uses different training methods. • Can be motivational. • Can link-in with phases of training. • Principles of training/ effective practice easily applied.

Knowing how to train

This will be evident in your selection of the most appropriate method(s) to match the fitness demands of the activity and/or the specific demands of the role/position played and be linked with your fitness strengths and weaknesses. Other training considerations relate to *managing* your training, which requires knowledge of training phases.

47

Summary

Different types of fitness

Why has it been important to learn about this **key concept**?

Learning about this **key concept** has a range of benefits:

1. You will be more knowledgeable about the importance of related fitness needs specific to selected activities and roles in performance.
2. You will be more knowledgeable about the different approaches you can use when training.
3. You will understand the importance of selecting specific training related to your needs and level of performance.
4. You will be able to link this understanding to make sense of other **key concepts** as you study the other **analysis areas**.

For example, you will be able to consider:

- the most suitable approach to use
- the most appropriate methods of training to use linked to your approach
- the benefits of each approach
- what you need to consider before selecting the most appropriate approach.

Using these strategies in the exam

Remember, in your exam you may be required to demonstrate your understanding of this **key concept** by recalling the information. In this instance, you could be asked to:

- Describe in detail the specific fitness demands of a particular role you played.

Alternatively you could be asked to demonstrate how you were able to make use of this acquired knowledge. For example, you could be asked to:

- Select one training approach and briefly describe a training programme. Discuss why it was appropriate for you to train using this method.

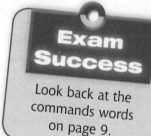

Exam Success

Look back at the commands words on page 9.

Quick Task

Choose an activity and think what would be the best training approach to use.

Select the most appropriate method(s) of training and describe a training session you carried out.

Take into account the fitness demands or the role you played.

Keep this as part of your study notes. It will help you to recall information more efficiently.

Improving your exam technique

Let us examine a past paper question and response.

This time you are looking at a description of a training programme with a selected approach to training. You are also asked to discuss why the selected approach was appropriate. The examiner is testing your knowledge of approaches to training.

Good exam technique

1. READ the question.
2. NOTE the mark value.
3. CONSIDER the **command word** (this has been embolden for you).
4. REFLECT on what the **command word** is telling you to do.

Sample question, answer and feedback

Question

Training can take place:

- within the activity (conditioning)
- outwith the activity
- through a combination of both.

Select one of the above and **discuss** why the approach selected was appropriate for developing your fitness in an activity from your course.
6 marks

Now read the sample answer

Note: the discussion word/phrase has been highlighted in yellow.

My activity is squash and I am going to discuss why training within the activity is appropriate. CRE and agility are two aspects of fitness that are required for effective performance in squash. The rallies can be long and so can games and matches. Agility is needed to reach all corners of the court and to be able to change direction quickly and get back to the 'T' for the next shot. Training to improve these aspects of fitness on the squash court is easily done. It is appropriate as the work done in training can involve squash specific movements and also racquet drills that develop both my fitness and the skills I need in the game. I did running routines and shadow drills returning to the 'T' each time. This focus on playing a shot and returning each time is relevant to the demands of the game and used squash-specific movements. I then did the same using a ball and practising different shots repeatedly until I made a mistake. I tried to keep the drills going for as long as possible. I was practising game situations by doing this. By doing these drills I am building up my agility and CRE as well as my range of shots. Training in this way on the court is appropriate in simulating the real fitness demands of match play where I have to try and keep playing in rallies. Training in the activity is also more fun and you are enthusiastic because you are practising ball play. I am also more motivated to keep working so pushing myself in terms of fitness and using skills. It is also enjoyable and because of this you can push yourself to improve.

Examiners' feedback

This is a clear and detailed response. The writer offers relevant knowledge of the approach selected and backs this up with relevant discussion as the appropriateness of the approach selected. The writer exhibits good analytical thinking.
6/6

Types of fitness

> **Key concept 3**
> Physical, skill-related and mental types of fitness.

The knowledge you will acquire from studying this **key concept** will help you understand about the types of fitness and aspects of fitness and how they relate to activities.

In any activity there are three types of fitness necessary to produce an effective performance.

- physical
- skill-related
- mental.

Each type comprises of related components. For example, a football player requires cardio-respiratory endurance (CRE, an aspect of physical fitness) co-ordination (an aspect of skill-related fitness) and managing emotions (an aspect of mental fitness) to perform effectively in a game.

Let us examine each type of fitness and consider the related components.

Physical fitness

This refers to the body's capacity to meet the varied demands of the activity for a sustained period. This requires the heart, lungs and muscles to function to maximum efficiency.

- Cardio-respiratory endurance (CRE)/aerobic/anaerobic endurance is the ability of the heart to deliver blood to the working muscles to produce effort for long periods of time. For example, in football, a midfield player, must be able to run effectively in both attack and defence positions.
- Aerobic endurance allows the body to work for long periods of time where the energy comes from oxygen. For example, long distance running or cycling or swimming. Think about your studies in Biology – the Krebs Cycle.
- Anaerobic endurance is where the energy is supplied without oxygen. For example a 100 metre sprint in athletics.

- Local muscular endurance is the ability for muscles to work repeatedly over a long time. For example in swimming, 400 metres front crawl – the arm and shoulder muscles produce sustained effort repeatedly to ensure an effective stroke.
- Strength/strength endurance is the ability of the muscles to exert force against an object or person. For example, in basketball, a centre when rebounding needs good strength to block out their opponent to prevent them getting the ball.
- Speed/speed endurance is the ability to move all or parts of the body as quickly as possible. For example, in badminton, speed endurance is essential to reach, retrieve the shuttle and get back to the T ready for the next shot. Rallies are often long and demanding and played at a fast pace.

- Power is a combination of strength and speed in explosive bursts of movement. For example, in shot putt, power ensures good distance.
- Flexibility is the ability of the joints to move through a full range of movement. For example a gymnast requires flexibility to execute the leg splits.

Importantly, all components of physical fitness often feature in combination to ensure effective performance. For example, a tennis player needs flexibility to be able to cover the court effectively, reach shots whilst requiring speed to cover the court quickly and demonstrate power during service and general court play.

Skill-related fitness

Components of skill-related fitness are shown below.

- Agility is the ability to move and change direction. For example, in swimming, agility is important in the tumble turn to effectively approach, plant and push off into the swim phase as fast as possible.
- Co-ordination is the ability of different parts of the body to work in unison to execute movements effectively. For example, in tennis, hand-eye co-ordination when serving is essential. At the toss-up, the eyes focus on the point of impact whilst the arms, shoulders, abdominals and back muscles impact the power to direct the ball.
- Reaction time is the ability to react to a stimulus; this could be auditory, sensory or tactile. For example, in the 100 metres, an athlete is required to react to the auditory stimuli of the gun firing and get out of the blocks fast into their stride pattern quickly.
- Balance is the ability to control the body's position when stationary or moving. For example, a gymnast needs good balance when performing a handstand by maintaining their centre of gravity over the base of support, i.e. their arms.
- Timing is the ability to perform skills at the correct time to meet the performance challenge. For example, in volleyball, a spiker must time their run up to execute an explosive jump to meet the ball at peak flight to impact power and placement.
- Movement anticipation is the ability to assess the performance challenge, predict what is going to happen next and select the appropriate decision to meet the challenge. For example, in football, the defender must watch the flight of the ball, anticipate his opponent's movement and beat them to the ball.

Importantly, all components of skill-related fitness often feature in combination to ensure effective performance. For example, in badminton agility is essential to cover the court effectively, enables quick changes of direction to reach, retrieve and then recover to the central position. Footwork requires good timing, coordination and movement to the shuttle; sub routines of preparation, action and recovery.

Mental fitness

It is often argued that what separates the top/elite performer from the rest is their mental toughness. The ability to handle pressure, control emotions, exhibit cool exterior and fight back, are all enviable characteristics of what makes the great GREAT!

- Mental rehearsal is the ability of the performer to visualise the PAR or sub-routines of the skill or action. For example, a golfer, playing an approach shot to the green rehearses the swing, flight path and ultimate direction of where the ball should land.
- Managing emotions is the ability to control feelings and deal with aggression. For example, in football referee decisions may be inaccurate; rulings are to accept decisions to offset yellow/red cards.
- Level of arousal is the body's ability to respond to physiological changes as a result of increased adrenalin into the blood stream. This may have a positive or negative effect on performance. For example, in a competition, previous experience/knowledge of results will affect the outcome. Recognising easy opponents may feature as under-arousal and complacency.

Importantly, all components of mental fitness often feature in combination to ensure effective performance. For example, in dance, before a competition the performer may consider the pressures of performing in front of an audience, thus pay more attention to mental rehearsal and visualize their routine. Attention to controlling emotions and keeping nerves in check may also feature.

It is important that you are familiar with at least one or two aspects of physical, skill-related and mental fitness and be able to describe or explain their importance within an activity or for a particular role that you are playing.

Summary

In the examples for each type of fitness there is acquired knowledge shown in the selection of the relevant aspects of fitness and then applied knowledge shown as to how these aspects are important for the activity chosen.

Physical, skill-related and mental types of fitness

Why has it been important to learn about this key concept?

Learning about this **key concept** has a range of benefits:

1. You will know the different types of fitness.
2. You will know the aspects that make up each type of fitness.
3. You will be able to link this understanding to make sense of other **key concepts** as you study the other analysis areas.

For example, you will be able to consider:

- the importance of aspects of fitness to particular activities
- the relationships between different aspects of fitness
- why certain aspects of fitness are specific to certain activities.

Using these strategies in the exam

Remember, in your exam you may be required to demonstrate your understanding of this **key concept** by recalling the information. In this instance, you could be asked to:

- describe the physical, skill-related and mental fitness requirements for effective performance within your activity
- select two types of fitness from the list below. Describe the importance of each type selected when performing in an activity:
  - physical fitness
  - skill related fitness
  - mental fitness.

Alternatively you could be asked to demonstrate how you were able to make use of this acquired knowledge. For example, you could be asked to answer the following:

- physical, skill-related and mental fitness are all required for successful performance – select an activity and explain why one aspect of each of these types of fitness is important.

Exam Success

Look back at the commands words on page 9.

Quick Task

Now you have been given some examples, from your own course select a type of fitness and describe in detail the aspects of fitness that are important for effective performance.

Keep this as part of your study notes. It will help you to recall information more efficiently.

Improving your exam technique

Let us examine a past paper question and response. The examiner is testing your knowledge of the particular type and aspects of fitness that are important for effective performance in a chosen activity.

Sample question, answer and feedback

Question

a) **Describe** the physical, skill-related and mental fitness requirements for effective performance within a chosen activity.

6 marks

Now read the sample answer

Note: the description word/phrase has been highlighted in blue.

The activity I have chosen is swimming. In swimming, cardio-respiratory endurance is important. Cardio respiratory endurance is the ability for the body to work for relatively long periods of time without becoming overtired. It is important that I can maintain my technique and breathing for as long as possible before I become tired. A high level of CRE will delay this process. It will also allow me to recover more quickly after the event.

Strength is also important as I am continuously working the muscles of the arm to generate propulsion to pull the body through the water. Strength is also important to push off the blocks at the start of a race.

In terms of skill-related fitness, coordination is important. This is the ability to work different parts of the body at the same time. In front crawl for example as one arm is pulling the opposite leg should be kicking downwards. Working legs and arms together help me produce the most efficient and effective stroke. Co-ordination is also important in breathing and helps reduce rotation and maintain a streamline position. The longer I can keep swimming with good technique through timing and co-ordination the more effective my stroke will be and hopefully get me a quicker time. I also need good reaction time so as soon as the gun or hooter goes I can push off the blocks and enter the water quickly and efficiently.

In swimming I require good concentration on things like stroke count to maintain a steady pace and keep my split times consistent. I also need concentration to keep my breathing steady and to achieve an effective turn at the end of each length and in the final swim to the finish. Managing my emotions is important when I am competing. I need to focus on what I am doing and be positive throughout a race and not let myself become anxious or distracted. By being focussed I can be in the correct frame of mind to perform well. I need to know what I am going to do in the race and forget about my opponents and spectators watching me. An effective stroke can lead to a faster time overall.

Examiners' feedback

This is a clear and detailed response. The writer offers good personal examples throughout the answer. There is clear evidence of each type of fitness and relevant aspects being described with relevance to the activity selected.

6/6

Top Tip

Practise giving this amount of detail in your answers and you are well on your way to a good pass.

Principles and methods of training

Key concept 4

Making sense of the principles and methods of training.

The knowledge you will acquire from studying this **key concept** will allow you to understand about the principles you require to apply to ensure your training programme is effective.

You will also learn about the different methods of training you can use to develop and improve your performance.

A good starting point is to immediately raise the question. What relevant principles must I apply to ensure a training programme is effective?

Specificity

The first key principle is specificity. Training has to be:

- Relevant to the activity; in particular the nature and fitness demands of the activity.
- Specific to individual needs. Data gathering will identify personal needs and the selected training programme must reflect this. For example, 'In football I identified from my data that my speed endurance was poor as the game wore on so I decided to plan a training programme specific to this need'. This could also relate to the specific needs you have in a particular role within the activity.

This approach will provide baseline evidence of fitness levels before training and aid future comparisons to be made.

Progressive overload

The second key principle is progressive overload. For a training programme to be effective it must be designed to place increasingly greater levels of demands on the body to ensure improvements.

Overload must be *progressive* to gradually increase the stress on the body/work rate/input. This is done by varying the following:

- Frequency; how *often*, vary the number of sessions per week, month or year. For example, 'I initially trained twice per week on a plyometric programme to improve my power for my long jump take off. After week 3 I applied overload by training three times per week.'
- Intensity; how *hard* or how *intense* the workload. For example when developing cardio-respiratory endurance your heart rate can be a measure of how hard you are working – when lifting weights increasing the number of repetitions or lifting heavier weights would be beneficial.
- Duration – how *long* is spent on each session. This depends on the specific individual/activity demands. It is recommended that training for a minimum of 6 weeks with 45–60 minutes per session is required to see improvement. Overload can be applied by increasing the time trained in any session.

- Rest and recovery – the amount of *time* between sessions or the recovery time between exercising. Each muscle requires adequate time to rest and recover between workouts. The actual duration of the rest and recovery period may vary from individual-to-individual based on factors such as their physical condition, diet, and the intensity of their training.
- Adaptation – dangers of *overtraining*; this can be avoided by adapting the frequency, duration and intensity of your training.

Reversibility

The final principle to consider is reversibility – in short 'use it or lose it'. When training stops, the *benefits* just acquired will diminish. Training loads will determine how long it takes for reversibility to happen.

Quick Task

Write up about the principles you considered when planning your training programme.

Keep this as part of your study notes. It will help you to recall information more efficiently.

Effective training methods

There are various methods of training that can be used to improve and develop physical, skill related and mental fitness.

Let us consider each of the following methods of training.

Physical fitness

Circuit training

Circuit training is a multi-station circuit of exercises. Each station is designed to address either the muscle groups to be used or specific type or aspect of fitness requiring development. Each exercise within the circuit is performed by repetitions or for a prescribed time before moving on to the next exercise. The exercises within each circuit are separated by brief, timed rest intervals, and each circuit is separated by a longer rest period. The total number of circuits performed during a training session may vary depending on your training level.

For example, to improve CRE a circuit comprising of astride jumps, squat thrusts, burpees, step-ups, press-ups, sit-ups and shuttle runs. Do each exercise for 30 seconds with a 30 second recovery between each exercise. Do three sets with a 3 minute rest between each set.

The advantages of using a circuit are:

- appropriate form of training for most sports
- can be adjusted to suit age, fitness and health of the athlete
- can develop general fitness as well as specific types or aspects of fitness
- a wide range of exercises to select from.

Weight training

This is the use of machine weights or free-standing weights. Working with various levels of resistance muscular endurance, power and dynamic and static strength can easily be addressed. There are two main types of weight training programmes. Isotonic weight training is the most common. This is when lifting weights the opposing muscles contracts and shortens and there is controlled movement. You usually use free standing weights. For example, to carry out a strength training programme you would work on specific exercises-chest press, leg press and squats. You might do three sets of eight reps working on 80% of your maximum lift. Isometric training is when the muscle contracts but does not shorten and requires muscle tension. An example would be pushing against a wall or lifting a dumbbell and holding it steady for a particular length of time.

The advantages of using weights are:

- can develop general fitness as well as specific types or aspects of fitness
- can develop muscular strength, power or muscular endurance
- can be used to develop specific muscle groups.

Fartlek

This involves short, fast runs or swims. Alternated with slow running or jogging recovery intervals. For example, long swim – set of continuous swimming, increasing speed for one to two lengths at a time.

The advantages of using Fartlek are:

- develops aerobic and anaerobic fitness.
- the individual can vary the intensity and plan to suit their demands.

Continuous

This involves exercising without rest intervals. Heart rates must be kept within training zone. For example, running for 20 minutes at a speed to keep your heart within training zone.

The advantages of using continuous are:

- improves cardio-respiratory endurance
- easy to carry out with no equipment needed
- develops aerobic fitness.

Interval training

This uses high-intensity work with alternating periods of rest. Rest periods are essential for the body to recover when hard work is undertaken. For example, swimming 6 × 50 metre sets with a minute's rest between each sets, then 6 × 50 metres sets with 45 seconds' rest.

The advantages of using interval training are:

- can develop aerobic and anaerobic fitness
- easy to apply overload
- allows you to train for longer periods of time.

Physical and skill-related training methods

Conditioning

This is training within the activity on physical fitness and at the same time developing the required activity skills. For example, in basketball, dribbling in and out of a set course of cones to improve agility as well as dribbling at speed.

The advantages of using conditioning training are:

- can improve skill-related and physical fitness
- can improve and develop skills in the activity
- enjoyable to do and can be motivational.

Mental fitness training methods

- Relaxation – releasing body tension to feel at ease and distract the mind from the activity/competition. For example, listening to music.
- Breathing – slow and deep breathing to relax and focus the mind to be composed and ready for performance. For example, during breathing think about being positive.
- Rehearsal – going over in the mind the precise movement/sequence of events for examples picturing the dance sequence from beginning to end or thinking of a quality performance.

Note: you will also study this information if you are examining the following: Performance Appreciation, **key concept** 4.

Summary

Principles and methods of training

Why has it been important to learn about this key concept?

Learning about this **key concept** has a range of benefits:

1. You will be more knowledgeable about the principles you require to apply when planning and developing a training programme.
2. You will be more knowledgeable about the relevant and appropriate training methods you can use to improve physical, skill-related or mental fitness.
3. You will be able to link this understanding to make sense of other **key concepts** as you study the other **analysis areas**.

For example, you will be able to consider:

- what key principles you need to apply to your training programme
- what each principle means
- the most relevant methods to make your training effective for types of fitness selected
- the appropriateness of each method of training.

Top Tip

Remember these are just a few examples. If you have understood this **key concept** then you will be able to offer more examples from your own experiences.

Using these strategies in the exam

Remember, in your exam you may be required to demonstrate your understanding of this **key concept** by recalling the information. In this instance, you could be asked to:

- explain the principles of training you would consider when designing a training programme.

Alternatively you could be asked to demonstrate how you were able to make use of this acquired knowledge. For example, you could be asked to:

- discuss how you applied the principles of training when carrying out your training programme.
- describe in detail one method of training you used to develop your fitness in your chosen activity.

or you could be asked to demonstrate how you were able to make use of this acquired knowledge. For example, you could be asked to:

- explain why the methods of training you used were appropriate.

Exam Success

Look back at the commands words on page 9.

Quick Task

Write up what method of training you used to develop your fitness in your chosen activity.

Keep this as part of your study notes. It will help you to recall information more efficiently.

Improving your exam technique

Let us examine two past paper questions. In question 1, you are looking at a discussion of related facts for 6 marks. Firstly, to help you make sense of how the examiner is testing your knowledge of the principles of training you have the opportunity to read part a) of the same question before considering the response to part b) of the question.

In question 2, you are looking at a description of a method of training and an explanation as to why your chosen method was appropriate. Firstly, to help you make sense of how the examiner is testing your knowledge of the methods of training, you have the opportunity to *read* parts a), b) and c) of the question, then *answer* part d).

Good exam technique

1. READ the question.
2. NOTE the mark value.
3. CONSIDER the **command word** (this has been embolden for you).
4. REFLECT on what the **command word** is telling you to do.

Sample questions, answers and feedback

Question 1

a) **Describe** how you assessed your fitness in an activity from your course. **Describe briefly** the main findings, referring to your future fitness needs.

b) **Discuss** how you applied the principles of training when planning a programme to meet your identified fitness needs.
6 marks

Top Tip

Practise giving this amount of detail in your answers and you are well on your way to a good pass.

Now read the sample answer

Note: the points referring to discussion have been highlighted in yellow.

When planning my training I took into account many factors and principles. The first principle I applied was specificity. I decided how long my training would last and which type of training would be most suitable. I made sure that the training was related to my identified needs and that the aspects of fitness I was improving were specific to the demands of the activity. I decided to use a progressive interval training programme and that it would be performance based within the activity. This would lead to an improvement in not only physical fitness but also my skill development. The next principles I took into account were frequency, duration and intensity. Because of the demands of the activity the minimum time for my programme would be six weeks, but as my main fitness was CRE, my programme would last near twelve weeks. I trained for four days a week with a rest day in between. Each session would last for about an hour. Within my training I made sure the intensity was 60–80% of my maximum effort and that I was working within my training zone in order to get maximum benefit. By checking my pulse rate regularly I would ensure this was the case.

In each session I had short rests so my body was not allowed to recover fully. The work ratio was initially 2:1 and eventually 3:1.

As my fitness level improved I applied the principle of progressive overload. This was done by gradually increasing the intensity of my training. Various methods were used to do this. I increased the number of sets and reps I was doing, the distance that I was swimming, the speed of the swim or the work rest ratio. By progressively overloading the body adapts and can cope with the new demands. In my case it lead to a higher level of CRE. I can now swim harder and longer before the build up of lactic acid, leading to deterioration in the effectiveness of the stroke.

The final principle I would apply was reversibility. If I stopped training I would lose the benefits I had just gained from the programme. I would try to maintain my level of fitness throughout the season even when I had stopped completely by gradually reducing the training.

Examiners' feedback

This is a clear and detailed response. The writer offers good personal examples of how the principles were applied with relevant discussion backed up with examples The writer exhibits good analytical thinking.

6/6

Question 2

a) **Describe** the physical, skill-related and mental fitness requirements for effective performance in your activity.

b) From the fitness requirements described in a), select one aspect. **Explain** how you gathered information about it within the activity.

c) There are three phases of training:

- preparation (pre-season)
- competition (during the season)
- transition (off season)

Discuss why your training might differ between each of the phases. Give examples to support your answer

d) **Describe** one method you used to develop your fitness. **Explain** why this method was appropriate.

4 marks

Top Tip

Practise giving this amount of detail in your answers and you are well on your way to a good pass.

Now read the sample answer

Note: the description word/phrase has been highlighted in blue. The points referring to explanation are highlighted in green.

The method of training I used was interval training. This method of training involved me working on periods of high intensity swimming trying to improve my CRE alternating with periods of rest. This work along with me resting in between allowed me to train for longer periods of time and therefore allowing me to gain greater benefits from my training. I started off with a warm-up then did some stroke/ technique work. I then did my main set which was 6 × 50 metre swim followed by a minutes rest between each set. I then did a subset of 6 × 50 metre swim with 45 seconds recovery between each set and then a warm-down to finish. Interval training is based on the principle of overload and can develop both aerobic and anaerobic fitness. When I am using interval training the hard work I am doing will ensure that my fitness level is progressing. It is also appropriate as I can vary the time or distance of each period of exercise or the amount of intensity I put in to each exercise or the recovery time or number of sets in each session therefore making it varied and enjoyable. Finally it is also appropriate as I can do this training within the swimming pool.

Examiners' feedback

This is a clear and detailed response. The writer offers a good description of a method of training used. The writer also gives detailed explanation as to the appropriateness of the method.

4/4

Planning effective training

> ### Key concept 5
> Planning, implementing and monitoring training in pursuit of personal goals.

The knowledge you will acquire from studying this **key concept** will help you understand about the different phases of training and their relationship to performance.

You will also reflect on the importance of planning and monitoring training using particular methods.

All activities have different playing seasons and consequently have varied training periods. For example, cricket has a short season whereas other activities such as football and rugby have much longer training periods.

The main objective of training is for the performer to peak and produce their best performance at particular times. To ensure this happens training must be well organised and planned for the year.

Periodisation is very important in planning training. This is where the training year is broken into periods of manageable time called 'phases' of training. There are three main phases which allow the performer to prepare, plan and manage their training programme for the main competition season or possibly the climax to a competition season.

Let us consider each of the phases.

Preparation or pre-season

During this phase of training you are concentrating on building up general aerobic endurance. You will be involved in general running/circuit training and working on particular drills that will develop the skills specific for the activity. Your training should relate to the demands of your activity so it will work on skill-related as well as physical fitness. It should also relate to your role within the activity. You will gradually build up the intensity of the training as you progress towards the competition period. For example, 'for my role as a guard in basketball I worked on a circuit to improve my CRE as well as working on a skills circuit to improve my passing and dribbling skills.'

Think about what you did pre-season for your sport.

Competition or in season

In this phase you are looking to maintain your level of fitness you have built up in pre-season. Emphasis now will be on fine-tuning skills, for example, shooting in netball, and working on particular strategies or plays that you will use in your activity, for example, working on a penalty corner routine in hockey or free kick in football. Depending on the activity, you may have to peak for a particular competition or match so there will be a tapering down period prior to this event to avoid training fatigue. You will reduce the amount you train and this will allow rest and recovery from your training programme.

Transition or off season

In this phase the body will be recovering after the competition period and allowing the body to recover. You, however, will want to try and maintain a reasonable general level of fitness. To achieve this you may take part in other activities, for example, cycling or swimming.

Using these strategies in the exam

Remember, in your exam you may be required to demonstrate your understanding of this **key concept** by recalling the information. In this instance, you could be asked to:

- select a phase of training
- describe the content of a training session you would do during this particular phase of training.
- discuss why your training might differ between each phase of training – give examples to support your answer.

Quick Task

Write up about what you did in the training programme and give details on how it differed during the season. Keep this as part of your study notes. It will help you to recall information more efficiently.

Planning, implementing and monitoring training

When planning a fitness programme it is important that a training programme:

- is specific to the demands of the activity in terms of fitness types to be developed
- meets the needs of the performer
- addresses the strengths and weaknesses of the performer
- takes into facilities account
- uses an appropriate and relevant method
- can be adapted according to the performer's rate of progress
- can be monitored and reviewed.

Note: this information is covered in more detail in Preparation of the Body, **key concepts** 3 and 4.

A typical plan for a training programme could be:

- collect, record and analyse data from performance
- identify fitness types or aspects to be developed
- select most appropriate method(s) of training
- carry out programme taking into account principles of training
- adapt or apply overload to programme
- monitor and review programme.

An important part of planning training is the consideration of short- and long-term goals. This will give a target to work towards to ensure optimal performance is reached at the correct time.

When planning and implementing your training programme it is important to monitor your training performance. Let us remind ourselves that monitoring means analysing and checking your performance on an ongoing basis. This is important for various reasons.

- It will provide both qualitative or quantitative details on whether your training is effective.
- It can show whether progress is being made.
- It can provide evidence to compare your performance at various stages of your training programme.
- It allows you to make changes and adapt your programme.
- It can show you whether the training method was appropriate and was at the correct intensity.
- It can promote motivation.
- It will show you whether the short-term and long-term goals have been achieved.

There are various ways of monitoring your programme.

- Video – for example, you could video your performance and compare to your initial performance.
- Observation schedules – for example, taking data on CRE in football to see how often you walked, jogged and sprinted during the latter stages of a game and comparing to previous data.
- Personal evaluation – saying how you feel throughout your training programme and if you think you are improving.
- Training diary – for example, keeping a note of how your training is going and what you did and the changes you made as the training progressed.
- Testing – for example, doing the same agility test and comparing the results to your previous results and to national norms.
- Game analysis – for example, taking statistics from a game and comparing them to the previous stats to see if there is a difference.

Note: you will have also studied this in more detail in Performance Appreciation, **key concept** 5.

Quick Task

Write up about the methods you used in your course to monitor your programme to see if was effective.

Keep this as part of your study notes. It will help you to recall information more efficiently.

Summary

Planning, implementing and monitoring

Why has it been important to learn about this key concept?

Learning about this **key concept** has a range of benefits:

1. You will know what phases make up a training year.
2. You will be more knowledgeable about how training differs in each training phase.
3. You will be able to link this understanding to make sense of other **key concepts** as you study the other **analysis areas**.
4. You will understand the importance of monitoring your training.
5. You will know what methods you could use to monitor your training.

For example, you will be able to consider:

- what you need to work on in each training phase
- how each phase differs in terms of what you work on
- the importance of each phase
- which are the best methods of monitoring your training.

Using these strategies in the exam

Remember, in your exam you may be required to demonstrate your understanding of this **key concept** by recalling the information. In this instance, you could be asked to:

- describe how you monitored the effectiveness of your training programme
- discuss why it is important to monitor your training programme.

Exam Success

Look back at the commands words on page 9.

Improving your exam technique

Let us examine two past paper questions. In question 1, you are given the names of the phases of training and asked to discuss why your training would differ between each of the phases, giving specific examples of what you did within your training programme.

In question 2, you are being asked to describe one method you used to monitor the effectiveness of your training programme. Firstly, to help you make sense of how the examiner is testing your knowledge of the methods of monitoring training it is important to *read* parts (a), (b) and (c) of the question, then *answer* part d).

Good exam technique

1. READ the question.
2. NOTE the mark value.
3. CONSIDER the **command word** (this has been embolden for you).
4. REFLECT on what the **command word** is telling you to do.

Sample question, answer and feedback

Question 1

There are three phases of training:

* preparation (pre-season)
* competition (during the season)
* transition (off season)

Discuss why your training might differ between each of the phases. Give examples to support your answer.

Now read the sample answer

Note: the description word/phrase has been highlighted in blue. The points referring to discussion are highlighted in yellow.

In the preparation phase of training I am trying to build up general fitness work and in particular my aerobic endurance. I could do this by running long slow distance runs twice per week to start with then gradually increasing this as I get nearer the competition phase. I could also do work like circuit training or particular drills. This means that I am increasing the intensity as I near this phase. The fitness work I am doing will remain specific to the demands of my event. I would also work on the skills I require for my activity. Whereas in the competition phase my fitness needs to be maintained, I would be looking to do quality training. In this phase I will have reached a particular level of fitness and will look upon to rely on the benefits I have gained from pre season. I would also work on specific aspects of fitness that I require for competition. In swimming I could be working on aspects of fitness, for example strength and speed endurance. I could work on a strength training programme by doing weights. In this phase I would swim in quite a few races and I would like to peak for these races so my training may increase in intensity for a while and then taper down before the competition. This tapering down allows my body to recover. Here I would decrease the frequency, duration and intensity of each session.

The difference in the final phase is that my body is now recovering after competitions and needs to recover. I would cut the training down in order to achieve this. However I would try to maintain a general and reasonable level of fitness. I could take part in other activities, for example I could do some cycling or golf or tennis. I would also cut down on the amount of time that I spend on training.

Examiners' feedback

This is a clear and detailed response. The writer discusses well the difference between the training in each phase with sound logical and analytical thinking shown. The examples given are relevant and enhance the answer given.   6/6

Question 2

a) Select two aspects of fitness. **Describe** in detail one situation where it was crucial to your performance.

b) **Explain** in detail the principles you took into account when planning your training programme to improve your fitness for your chosen activity.

c) At times you will have made changes to your programme. Give two examples of the changes you made and **explain** why these changes were necessary.

d) **Describe** one method you used to monitor the effectiveness of your training programme. **Explain** why this method was appropriate.

Now read the sample answer

Note: the description word/phrase has been highlighted in blue. The points referring to explanation are highlighted in green.

The method that I used to monitor the effectiveness of my training was to keep a training and performance diary. After each training session I made a brief record of the work completed and then recorded how I had felt both during and at the end of each session. This helped me monitor whether the intensity of the training was about right and allowed me to comment on how I felt my fitness was developing. For example, at the end of week 3 of cross court 3v3, I recorded that I was now rebounding effectively in defence right throughout until the end of the third 10-minute game. I also made records in the diary how I had felt physically during and after each of our school games. I had made specific reference to the effectiveness of my CRE and rebounding. This was an effective method in that it gave me a chance to consider how I felt the training programme was benefiting my whole performance as a centre and reflected on my training and performance goals.

Examiners' feedback

This is an answer where the writer gives a clear description of the method used to monitor the training. The explanation of the appropriateness of the method is well explained and shows relevant knowledge.   4/4

Skill and skilled performance

> **Key concept 1**
> The concept of skill and skilled performance.

Remember in this **analysis area** you will be studying information that will help you to look at **specific** parts of your performance.

The **specific** focus incorporates your ability to understand the nature of skill, skilled performance, stages of learning, methods of practise and factors that will influence your performance development.

The knowledge you will acquire from studying this key concept will help you to understand about the different types of skills that contribute to effective performances.

Ability and skill

A good starting point is to consider what we mean by *ability* and *skill*.

Ability is your genetic potential, i.e. your *inherent talent* to do something well – jump high, sprint fast, throw far, etc.

Skill is a learned process; this requires you to take-in instruction, reflect on what you have done well, reflect on what you can do to further refine and make your performance better. This requires commitment, dedication and a desire to succeed.

The next crucial point is to understand what the terms *skills* and *techniques* mean. Although used interchangeably they mean very specific things.

• Skill refers to the end result of practise and reflects your ability to select and apply the correct technique to suit the immediate challenge.
• Techniques are concerned with *why*, *when* and *how effectively* performers execute them.

Let us consider Barbara Knapp's work who defines skill as follows:

'A skill is the learned ability to bring about pre-determined results with maximum certainty, often with the minimum outlay of time or energy or both.'

A more simplistic overview is achieving the end result reliably and on demand rather than haphazardly or down to good luck.

A learned ability – the netball player has to *learn* how to perform an overhead shot.

Pre-determined results – the netball player *sets out* to put the ball in the net.

Maximum certainty – the netball player *expects* to put the ball into the net every time.

Maximum efficiency – the netball player will *appear* to make the shot look effortless, with little energy required and apparently lots of time to do it.

This level of perfection takes years of dedicated practice – this is the definition of *experience*.

So when we refer to someone being skilled, it is not just about carrying out a set of movements efficiently but also relies on the performer being knowledgeable about the rules, fit for the demands of the activity, and in control of mental attitudes to apply strategies in context of the performance.

In short, a skilled performance is about the interplay between *intention* and *action*.

Categories of skill

Skills *are learned*, and can be sub-divided into two categories:

Physical skills

Also known as motor skills, these form the basis of all sports and are classed as two types.

- Simple motor skills. These require very little intricate body movement and are similar in most sports. Examples include: running, jumping, throwing, catching etc.
- Complex motor skills. These require intricate body movements with finer control of many body parts. For example, the lay-up shot in basketball, a long arm overswing in gymnastics etc.

Mental skills

All performances in sport require some form of mental activity.

- The simple motor skills (see above), require little mental input, whereas activities such as orienteering require the performer to mentally assess the situation before making a decision about the next move. This is referred to as *information processing*.
- Mental input is required to 'read the game' also known as *scanning*. For example, knowing when to spike in volleyball in preference to playing a dump shot to out-manoeuvre opponents.
- Working out why errors occurred during a performance requires a high level of mental input. For example, I should have hit that ball slower/faster.

Skilled performers exhibit a wide range of the skills referenced above. High levels of all-round fitness are evident as they produce flawless application and remain in control of their emotions, performing with composure.

Note: Recognising and understanding the benefits of a skilled performance will help you develop your own performance, as you need to link this knowledge when designing a practice development programme. You will also study this information in Performance Appreciation, **key concept** 4 and Preparation of the Body **key concept** 3.

Skill classification

Skills are classed into various categories. This is known as *skill classification*.

Open skills

The environment, for example, wind, sun, rain or the terrain can affect the performance of a skill. Skills affected by the environment are known as open skills and are found in activities that involve opponent(s).

Wherever there is an element of unpredictability then the skills can be classified as open. This is also referred to as being externally paced, i.e. external factors determine when the skill or performance is carried out, for example, a centre pass in netball or an attempt at goal in football.

Closed skills

These are skills where an opponent's actions play very little or no part in the performance of a skill and skills where the performer is in almost total control of their performance. The physical environment does not affect closed skills either. Closed skills are referred to as being self-paced, i.e the performer decide when they are going to perform the skill, for example, hitting a golf ball.

It is important to remember that some skills will fall between these extremes. This is known as a *continuum* between open skills and closed skills.

- Discrete skills – skills that are self-paced and have a distinct start and finish, for example, long jump.
- Serial skills – skills that link a group of discrete skills to make a new complex execution skill, for example, triple jump.

Mental skills – information processing

Learning new skills and then having the ability to select and apply these skills depends on your ability to *process information*. You develop this ability by making sense of the information received from a stimulus via muscle translation – your brain sending messages to appropriate muscle groups and storing this in your memory. When facing similar performance challenges you are able to retrieve this information and make appropriate decisions.

Look at the diagram below. This shows how you process information when *learning* a skill or technique. The table shows how you process information when *applying* skills in performance situations – notice all the different types of stimuli that need to be processed for success.

Note: as you become more experienced you will learn to select the relevant information from the irrelevant information on display to ensure you are effective – this takes years of practice.

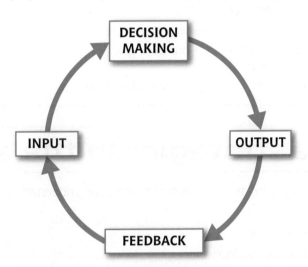

INPUT	DECISION MAKING	OUTPUT	FEEDBACK
This could come from: – watching the ball – watching opponent – looking for support – from a call/shout The brain also receives information from joints and limbs (kinaesthetic sense) *The sense of touch plays a part.* * * Relevant information is selected, interpreted and then used to make decisions. The memory and previous experiences are used in this process of decision making.	Experience plays a part in selecting the correct information. The more experienced player, the easier they sort out the important information. The information that is used is linked with experiences stored in our memory. e.g. THINK ABOUT a basketball player watching an opponent shoot. The player – TAKES ACCOUNT of speed and direction of the ball. On flight to the ring – JUDGES the shot will be too strong and will rebound from the backboard. The player DECIDES to move into position in line with where the ball will rebound from the backboard AT THE SAME TIME considers how to get to it before others.	When we react to a situation, our nervous system sends messages to the muscles about the movement needed. This is a complex process; * * e.g. to judge the correct force, the right timing, the direction of the action. THINK ABOUT the player who has now secured the rebound – and denied the offensive player opportunity to shoot again. AT THE SAME TIME releases an outlet pass to start an offence move.	Was the outlet pass successful? Yes - then move to fill channel and assist play No - then delay opponent's play

Summary

Skill and skilled performance

Why has it been important to learn about this **key concept**?

Learning about this **key concept** has a range of benefits:

1. You will be more knowledgeable about the notion of skill – able to identify the factors that contribute to skilled performance.
2. You will be able to link this understanding to make sense of other key concepts as you study the other analysis areas.
3. You will broaden your appreciation of performance development from a sports science perspective.

For example, you will be able to consider:

- the different types of skill and how they are executed
- the impact of skill learning and information processing
- how skilled performances are perfected
- the importance of feedback when learning and applying skills.

Top Tip

Remember these are just a few examples. If you have understood this **key concept** then you will be able to offer more examples from your own experiences.

Using these strategies in the exam

Remember, in your exam you may be asked to demonstrate your understanding of this **key concept** by *recalling* the information.

In this instance, you could be asked to:

- describe the features of a skilled performance
- describe the difference between simple and complex, open and closed, discrete and continuous or serial skills.

Alternatively you could be asked to demonstrate how you were able to make use of this acquired knowledge. For example, you could be asked to:

- discuss skills' classification or information processing when learning or developing your skill
- explain why it is important to consider skill types when planning a practice programme.

Exam Success

Look back at the commands words on page 9.

Quick Task

Write up how effectively you focus and remain calm when performing. Would others agree with your opinion? Keep this as part of your study notes. It will help you to recall information more efficiently.

Improving your exam technique

Let us examine a past paper question and response. This time you are looking at a discussion of related facts for 6 marks. Firstly, to help you make sense of how the examiner is testing mental factor understanding, you have the opportunity to *read* part a) of the same question before *answering* part b).

Sample questions, answers and feedback

Question

Choose an activity and a skill or technique.

a) **Describe** the features of a skilled performance in this activity. 4 marks

b) When learning or developing a skill or technique, **discuss** the importance of one of the following: 4 marks

- information processing
- skill classification

Now read the sample answer

Note: the description word/phrase has been highlighted in blue; when an explanation has been offered this has been highlighted in yellow.

I know that information processing involves reaction to a stimulus, i.e. the brain sends a message to the muscles to ensure action takes place. The brain makes sense of the action taken and the whole process starts again. This diagram shows how it works.

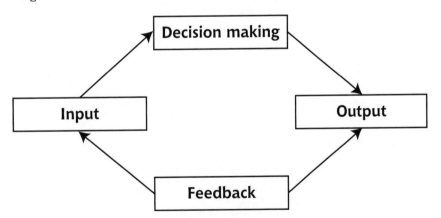

I know when I am learning skills that this process happens extremely quickly with all four parts linked together. At the input stage it is important that I pay great attention as this is when I receive information (known as stimulus or cue); this could be an instruction from my coach or movement by my team-mate/opponent. Secondly, based on this information I must make sense of this, i.e. take on board what I have been told or seen and make a decision about what action I am going to make. Thirdly, at the output stage I need to respond to the information given and produce 'an action'. The last part is extremely important as this is where I receive feedback on how effective my action or decision was – for example, did I execute the skill appropriately? – based on this outcome the whole success starts again instantaneously. This feedback can be given externally/internally and often a combination of both.

I have learned that this is a continuous process and the more experienced you are the better you are at it. It takes lost of practice to develop and good performers can do it automatically. Information processing relies on the person's ability to take on information and act on it – as they get better they need less external feedback and can more accurately act upon on internal feedback when learning skills.

Previous experience and complexity of the skill counts for a lot because at different times you may need to rely more heavily on instruction or demonstration before you are successful in learning and then able to apply the skill.

Examiners' feedback

This is a clear and detailed response. The writer understands about the information processing. Relevant and detailed information/diagram is given to support points raised.

The writer exhibits good critical thinking.   4/4

Top Tip

Practise giving this amount of detail in your answers and you are well on your way to a good pass.

Analysing, monitoring and reviewing skills and techniques

> **Key concept 2**
> Skill and technique improvement through mechanical and movement analysis or consideration of quality.

The knowledge you will acquire from studying this key concept will help you understand about the assessment process, i.e. the purpose of gathering information and making sense of the findings.

Any assessment of skill movement must begin with the question 'why in the first place?'

Due to the complex nature of sport – continuous, dynamic and fast action, it is difficult, if not impossible, to observe and remember the entire key points occurring within a performance. Yet analysis based on accurate *observation* and *recall* is essential for improving performance.

Analysis and evaluation

To do this successfully depends on your ability to *assemble information, sort it, evaluate it and draw conclusions from it*. This is known as the process of *anlaysis and evaluation*.

Analysis

This primarily involves examining a piece of data, a table, observation checklist, chart or diagram and making some sense out of it; in other words, *interpreting the results*. It may also involve identifying certain elements that make up the problem: *diagnostic analysis – making an attempt to explain cause and effect.*

The effectiveness of performance analysis relies on the accuracy of observation and making it understandable or intelligible to another person.

Evaluation

This involves judgement and opinion about how important, significant and effective skill improvement has been. Making such judgements implies that there are no wrong or right answers but what is important is that judgements made need to be supported/substantiated. Valid and reliable methods of gathering information are available for this purpose (for an explanation about validity and reliability issues see page 29–30).

It is important to use a *systematic* approach when gathering information. The first critical step is *to define* the purpose. In relation to this analysis area the *purpose* is your ability to select and apply skill effectively to meet performance demands.

By selecting from movement analysis, mechanical analysis and consideration of quality you will have:

- evidence related to your whole performance (initial/general/primary data)
- evidence related to specific parts of your performance (focussed/specific/secondary data).

This will help you to:

- identify performance strengths and weaknesses
- set personal goals
- plan practice strategies/programmes
- evaluate change over a period of time
- receive and act upon feedback (the most important contributor to affect learning and subsequent performance of a skill)
- predict future performance.

Logical and critical thinking skills are tested here as you are required to justify the appropriateness of your preferred selection. In addition, you must also be able to justify the *limitations* of methods selected, for example, human error, lack of activity-specific knowledge on behalf of the recorder, time constraints etc.

The methods in the following table are considered both valid and reliable for the purposes of analysing, monitoring and review of related skills and techniques. All are excellent sources of external feedback. Understanding the specific benefits of each will enable you to select wisely when examining your own performance strengths and weaknesses.

MOVEMENT ANALYSIS	MECHANICAL ANALYSIS	CONSIDERATION OF QUALITY
Supports analysis of: • basic movement patterns • court coverage/shot placement • sub routine identification of preparation/action and recovery. Best suited for activities such as, football, basketball, badminton etc.	Supports analysis which: • looks at force • body levers • balance/rotation/propulsion. Best suited for activities like gymnastics, athletics, swimming.	Supports analysis of: • the control/precision • the flair/effort • timing/co-ordination. Suited for all activities.

Methods of gathering information

METHODS	BENEFITS
Digital recording methods • Video tape • Digital photography • Computer programmes	The most reliable for obvious reasons; free from human bias, replay facilities, provides a permanent record, easy comparisons, motivating. Qualitative/quantitative/diagnostic feedback on whole performance and/or skills in isolation.
Player profile – record sheets/checklists • A movement analysis • Could be a consideration of quality	Permanent record, easy to use, more than one can be used at any one time. Qualitative/quantitative feedback on skills in isolation.
Questionnaires, record sheets • Could be a consideration of quality	Permanent record, easy to use, more than one can be used at any one time. Qualitative feedback on whole performance and/or skills in isolation.
Scattergram – diagram of ... • Could be movement analysis	Permanent record, easy to use, more than one can be used at any one time. Qualitative/quantitative feedback.
Standardised tests – record sheets • Could be movement analysis	Permanent record, easy to use, compared against norms, more than one can be used at any one time. Quantitative feedback on skills in isolation.
Match analysis sheets • Could be movement analysis	Permanent record, more than one can be used at any one time. Quantitative/diagnostic feedback on whole performance and/or skills in isolation (time related).

Observation checklists – PAR • Could be movement analysis or mechanical analysis	Permanent record, easy to use, compared to performance criteria and model performer, more than one can be used at any one time. Qualitative/diagnostic feedback on skills in isolation.
Flowcharts – graphs or notation sheets • Could be movement analysis or mechanical analysis	Permanent record, easy to use, more than one can be used at any one time. Quantitative feedback on skills in isolation.
Dictaphone – verbal commentary	Permanent record, easy to use, expert feedback offered, e.g. from coach. Qualitative/diagnostic feedback on whole performance and or skills in isolation.

It is important to remember once the information is gathered, careful interpretation of the results is necessary to plan practice programmes that will address the weaknesses prioritised for improvement. In addition, on completion of any practice or programme followed, the same methods of data will be examined for purposes of monitoring and review.

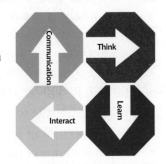

A point to consider

'When your writing is filled with detail, it has a lot more impact.'

Ivan Levison

Summary

Skill and technique improvement

Why has it been important to learn about this **key concept**?

Learning about this **key concept** has a range of benefits:

1. You will be more knowledgeable about reliable and valid methods of gathering information.
2. You will be able to link this understanding to make sense of other **key concepts** as you study the other **analysis areas**.
3. You will broaden your appreciation of performance development from a sports science perspective.

For example, in each **analysis area** you will be required to work with many types of data gathering. Your logical and critical thinking will become evident depending on the selection made, i.e 'what is the most appropriate method – justify *why?*'

You will also be able to consider

- the importance of feedback
- the importance of monitoring and review.

When referring to *Qualitative, Quantitive, Diagnostic types* of external feedback – what do we mean?

- Qualitative refers to the effectiveness of the skill/performance in terms of control, consistency, style or flair. For example, *my overhead clear is consistent, fluent and I have a powerful action*
- Quantitive refers to measurements, e.g. how many. For example, *7/10 of my overhead clears were played deep into back court.*
- Diagnostic identifies what is wrong with the skill/performance or offers a solution as to how to remediate or refine the skill/performance. For example, *taking the shuttle earlier and more in front of the head will help improve the contact and make the shot more powerful.*

Using these strategies in the exam

Remember, in your exam you may be asked to demonstrate your understanding of this **key concept** by *recalling* the information.

In this instance, you could be asked:

- describe the methods you used to gather information about your performance strengths and weaknesses
- describe the methods you used to monitor/review/evaluate your performance on completion of your training.

Alternatively you could be asked to justify your selection. In this instance you could be asked to

- discuss why the methods selected were appropriate
- offer a brief description followed by your explanation.

Exam Success

Look back at the commands words on page 9.

Quick Task

Make a list of the methods of data you have used. Describe the types of information that this allowed you to gather. Can you justify your choice?

Keep this as part of your study notes. It will help you to recall information more efficiently.

Improving your exam technique

Let us examine a past paper question and response. This time you are looking at a description with detailed explanation of related facts for 6 marks.

Sample question, answer and feedback

Question

Describe, in detail, the methods you used to gather information on your level of performance. **Explain** why these methods were appropriate.   6 marks

Top Tip

Practise giving this amount of detail in your answers and you are well on your way to a good pass.

Now read the sample answer

Note: the description word/phrase has been highlighted in blue and when an explanation has been offered this has been highlighted in green.

The data methods I used included the video, match analysis sheets and specific questionnaire sheet.

I wanted to find out how effective I was in my role as a hooker in rugby. Specifically, I wanted to know if I performed my defending and attacking duties consistently throughout the game. I decided to use the video as this was the best tool of analysis to avoid human error. The game is fast-paced and I did not want to miss anything. The video allowed me to look at my game several times, which let me check my match analysis and questionnaire sheets to see if they backed up what I was seeing. I could also discuss with my teammates and coach afterwards and get their expert opinions.

The match analysis was time related and divided into 5-minute sections for each half. I asked my marker to indicate the number of passes I made or intercepted, the number of tackles I made, the number of times I forced my opponent to the ground and to count the scrum support that I offered, etc.

My questionnaire was designed specifically to evaluate my mental skill. The specificity of the questions related to my success rate at controlling my temper; especially after making unforced errors or when the score was tight.

All these methods were appropriate as I was able to look at my strengths and weaknesses in my performance. Also I could discuss with my coach ways I could improve for example, I could then use this feedback to set targets for improvements. Using these methods was appropriate as I could compare my performance in the future once I had practised. I also found them to be very motivating and easy to use. The close-angle viewing of my scrummaging meant that I could refine my technique and try harder to perfect it. As I had used more than one method and gathered information from a variety of sources I felt that my information was reliable.

Examiners' feedback

This is a clear and detailed response. The writer understands about the appropriateness of data gathering with sound explanation offered to support choice selection.

The writer exhibits good critical thinking.   6/6

The three identifiable stages of learning

> **Key concept 3**
> The development of skill and the refinement of technique.

The knowledge you will acquire from studying this **key concept** will help you understand about the skill development process. This incorporates a study of the stages of learning, methods of practice, principles of effective practice and factors affecting performance.

Firstly, you need to understand about the three identifiable *stages of learning*. This will help select the appropriate *methods of practice* to effect change in your performance.

1. The cognitive (or preparation) stage.
2. The associative (or practice) stage
3. The autonomous (or automatic) stage

When learning, practising or refining skill, the demands on the performer are different at each of the three stages.

COGNITIVE STAGE	ASSOCIATIVE STAGE	AUTOMATIC STAGE
The performer needs to: • get a mental picture of the skill or technique • understand the basics of what is to be learned • break the skill down, if possible slow the skill down • receive instruction in small chunks • get a lot of corrective feedback.	The performer can: • understand what is expected therefore the focus shifts more on how to do it better • handle more specific information • attempt to recognise and correct own errors *(kinaesthetic awareness)* • make more sense of external feedback from model performers or coach.	The performer can: • select and apply skills without conscious thought • detect own errors and often refine or adapt immediately to manage the performance challenge • concentrate more on tactics, strategy and decision making.
Movements are often clumsy, jerky with patterns of skill movement fragmented. The attention demands are high because the learner uses a lot of conscious processing of information simply to perform and co-ordinate the movement.	Movements are more consistent with anticipation, timing and more complex skills evident in the performance.	Movements are highly consistent performed with precision, flair and fluency. Complex skills are handled effortlessly with little conscious thought to meet the various performances' demands.

Practice considerations

A good starting point is to remember that practice is the process of going through a movement without guidance; training on the other hand is the process of learning with guidance. Importantly, skill proficiency is due to effective learning, i.e. learning that allows permanent change.

Skill proficiency can only be enhanced if practice sessions are structured according to an individual's stage of learning, identified performance goals and the impact of feedback.

Types of practice

The next question to consider is what types of practice would be most beneficial to ensure the correct learning experiences. The following considerations should be made in relation to how to practice for example:

- all at once (known as *massed practice*, i.e. when the rest periods are short)
- in short periods (known as *distributed practice*, i.e. when the rest periods are frequent).

Once this initial decision has been made, the next consideration, within these blocks of time, is whether to practice using:

- the whole/part/whole approach
- the gradual build-up approach.

Whole/part/whole practice involves practising the whole skill as a complete action or movement. For example, front crawl technique – either breathing, arm and leg action at the same time or divide the technique and focus on breathing only, arm action only, leg action only and then recombine to whole action/movement.

Gradual build-up practice involves seeing a demonstration of the whole technique, then gradually introducing parts of the technique to bring about success before attempting full action/movement. For example, when a technique is particularly complex or dangerous, such as front spike in volleyball.

Methods of practice

The next logical step is to consider the various methods of practice available. Understanding the specific benefits of these methods will ensure practice brings about change.

METHODS OF PRACTICE	BENEFITS
Shadow – involves repeatedly shadowing the action.	Particularly useful at cognitive and associative stages of learning. Groove the pattern or rehearse movement patterns. Develops kinaesthetic awareness. Corrects error. Success gains high. Increases confidence and motivation.
Repetition – involves executing technique repeatedly. This can be performed as individual, pair or group.	Useful at cognitive and associative stages of learning. Reinforces sub phases of preparation, action and recovery. Enables performer to concentrate on one specific technique at a time. Enables practice to be uninterrupted or completed without fear of failure. Rest periods can be controlled. Increases confidence and motivation.
Combination – involves linking more than one skill and repeating sequential execution.	Useful at associative and autonomous stages of learning. Develops or refines more than one skill at a time. Reinforces skill replication in terms of consistency, accuracy and fluency. Introduces variety to practice. Increases motivation.
Pressure – involves executing technique in random or varied situations.	Useful at associative but mainly at autonomous stages of learning. Develops consistent application of techniques in game-like conditions. Improves decision making. Increases challenge.
Problem solving – involves selecting and executing range of techniques to match challenge.	Mainly at autonomous stages of learning. Develops consistent application of techniques in game-like conditions. Improves decision making. Increases challenge and enables techniques to be adapted.
Conditioned – involves executing technique in agreed and controlled manner.	Mainly at autonomous stages of learning. Develops consistent application of techniques in game-like conditions. Improves decision making. Enables techniques to be adapted. Highly challenging.

Planning considerations

Performers must be given the opportunity to learn techniques, develop skills and apply these in a variety of realistic situations. Practice sessions and programmes therefore need to be planned in a progressive manner. The specific aims and needs of the performer are crucial for development to occur; this is referred to as *goal setting*.

Goal setting

This provides the framework for achieving potential. Importantly, long-term goals should be established (what do I want to achieve?) with short-term goals interlinked (how am I going to get there?).

All performers need a sense of purpose and immediacy to ensure they remain focussed and motivated to do well in the longer term. To ensure goals are set appropriately the principles of effective practice must feature as an integral part of planning training. The acronym SMARTER will help you to remember these principles.

Goals must be:

S – specific to the performers' stage of learning, activity or task.

M – measurable: this will help the performer assess progress.

A – agreed: usually set between performer and coach to ensure selection of relevant practice methods.

R – realistic: this ensures sufficient challenge and promotes motivation; goals set must not be too easy or too difficult.

T – time-phased: this relates to the agreed time to reach a target or goal. This ensures progression.

E – exciting: this keeps the performer motivated to succeed; a sense of achievement and increased confidence.

R – recorded: this ensures commitment and allows monitoring and evaluation to take place.

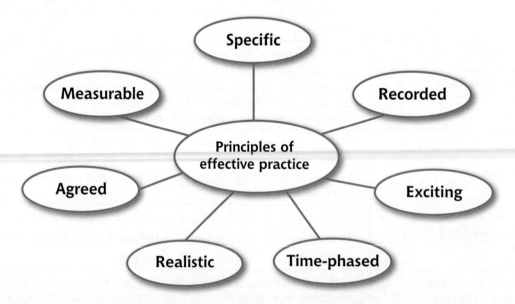

Factors affecting skill learning

Hopefully you will have recognised that skill learning may be viewed as a gradual process striving towards perfect performance.

The importance of feedback

The most important aid to the learning process is *feedback*. Feedback is the information received by the learner before, during or after skilled movement has been attempted; often viewed as the interaction between practice and performance.

There are two main types of feedback:

- intrinsic (*internal* – what you know and feel yourself)
- extrinsic (*external* – information gained from other sources – verbal, visual, written, kinaesthetic, vestibular); often referred to as 'knowledge of results' and 'knowledge of performance.'

Depending on the nature of the task/stage of learning/ goal set, learners may be able to improve their performance from intrinsic feedback alone. However, sometimes improvements are difficult, if not impossible, without extrinsic feedback. Without input from coach/teacher/model performer *(external)* the learner relies only on their own models of skill as a basis for error identification and correction *(internal/kinaesthetic)*. As a result *bad habits* may be formed with improvements slow.

For example, consider the different sources of feedback that the learner would require when learning how to swim front crawl, complete a back-hand block or a front somersault in trampolining.

Feedback is important as it informs of progress. This should be immediate, positive, clear and constructive. Note the three distinct purposes to:

1. Motivate you to increase efforts to achieve goals set.
2. Change performance by indicating either directly or indirectly the kinds of things you should do to refine movement patterns and correct errors.

   This information may be considered as:

   - qualitative – statements that reflect the quality of control, precise, effort, flair, creativity etc.
   - quantitive – statements that reflect the consistency and accuracy.

3. Reinforce learning, which lets you know that progress is being made.

Remember, for feedback to be of value you must:

- interpret the information offered
- process the information received; retrieve from memory
- compare against a reference, e.g. model performer/previous own performance.

The importance of motivation

This reflects on your decisions to take part and persevere in the many hours of practice often required. Motivation is the factor often considered crucial for the desire to succeed during performance as well as the variability in skill execution/application from one performance to another.

There are two main types of motivation:

- intrinsic (*internal* – how you push yourself to achieve goals set, self fulfilment and set new targets)
- extrinsic (*external* – you only respond to rewards or react to incentives, for example, medals, praise or prestige).

Intrinsic and extrinsic motivation can be viewed as *reinforcement* to learning. Often both are linked, however learning as a whole is reflected in a change from your dependency on extrinsic sources of motivation to internally generated sources; considered as the more influential with longer lasting results.

Motivation is the key to productive learning and relates to your perception in achieving goals. If you are highly motivated you devote more effort to the task, are more conscientious in training and willing to train for longer.

Motivational levels are linked to your:

- personality traits
- aspirations
- ability to deal with expectations from others
- experiences of success/failure
- ability to receive and act upon feedback offered.

The effort, intensity and direction you take in most cases is to achieve mastery of the skill, to surpass others, to improve self confidence and to gain social approval/admiration from family and friends.

It is important to remember therefore that your training programme needs to be challenging, interesting and geared towards achieving realistic goals.

The importance of concentration

This reflects your ability to focus on task-related information. Concentration is an internal process and is susceptible to factors such as mood, fatigue, boredom, anxiety, motivation, processing information and stages of learning.

Skill learning success is very dependent on mental activity, i.e. your ability to focus on the instruction, and or observe movement, assimilate what is being demanded of you (*then store to memory*) and produce action (*retrieve from memory*) to address the performance challenge.

During practice you will be learning how to build a repertoire of skills to meet varied performance challenges. Practice serves no useful purpose if you are unable to concentrate on the key elements about *how* to perform a skill.

For example, at the cognitive or associative stage of learning, when practising the v-sit or high scissor balance in gymnastics, specific attention will be geared towards achieving the *muscular feelings* gaining a *mental picture* of the preparation, action and recovery of technique. At this stage there is no real concentration on how it looks.

However, at the automatic stage, greater attention to perception, anticipation and decision-making will be evident about how to apply or adapt technique to make it look spectacular. To produce this skilled action requires you to process information (pay attention to relevant cues, i.e. where on the beam/horse you are) and retrieve from your stored memory the correct technique (I used the v-sit balance/horizontal crucifix kick to gain more points).

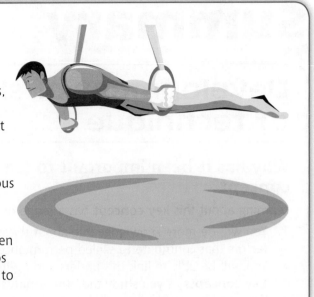

As you become more experienced you learn to ignore irrelevant cues, for example, noise from the crowd, previous low scores from judges etc.

Experience, motivation and self-confidence contribute to your ability to remain focussed and concentrate, both when refining and when applying skill in performance; this helps detect errors and reduces unforced errors and contributes to your repertoire of skills.

A point to consider

'We all have dreams. But in order to make dreams into reality, it takes an awful lot of determination, dedication, self-discipline, and effort.'

Jesse Owens

Summary

Development of skill and refinement of technique

Why has it been important to learn about this key concept?

Learning about this **key concept** has a range of benefits:

1. You will be more knowledgeable about the notion of skill – able to identify the factors that contribute to skilled performance.
2. You will be able to link this understanding to make sense of other **key concepts** as you study the other **analysis areas**.
3. You will broaden your appreciation of performance development from a sports science perspective

For example, you will be able to consider:

- the different stages of learning
- the selection of relevant practice methods and applying practice principles
- the importance of goal setting
- the different factors that affect performance.

Top Tip

Remember these are just a few examples. If you have understood this **key concept** then you will be able to offer more examples from your own experiences.

Using these strategies in the exam

Remember, in your exam you may be asked to demonstrate your understanding of this **key concept** by *recalling* the information.

In this instance there is a considerable depth about what you may be asked, for example:

- describe the features of a skilled performance
- describe the stages of learning
- describe the methods of practice you considered.

Alternatively you could be asked to demonstrate how you were able to make use of this acquired knowledge. For example, you could be asked to:

- discuss the methods of practice you used to develop ...
- explain the relevance of the methods used
- discuss the importance of feedback, motivation, concentration.

Exam Success

Look back at the commands words on page 9.

Quick Task

If a beginner came to you for advice on how to improve their ability to do a task, what advice would you give them? In respect of your own skill development, how important was the influence of feedback, motivation and concentration?

Keep this as part of your study notes. It will help you to recall information more efficiently.

Improving your exam technique

Let us examine a past paper question and response.

This time you are looking at a discussion of related facts for 6 marks. Firstly, the examiner is testing methods of practice understanding in part b), and in part c) of the same question the examiner is testing your understanding of influential factors for 6 marks.

Sample question, answer and feedback

Question

a) **Describe, in detail**, two different methods of practice you used to develop your performance of the skill or technique identified. **Explain** why you considered each of the practice methods selected to be appropriate.   6 marks

b) From the list below, select two of the factors that are influential in skill development. **Discuss** how each of the factors chosen affected the development of your skill or technique during practice.   6 marks

- motivation
- feedback
- anxiety
- concentration
- confidence

Now read the sample answer to part a

Note: the description word/phrase has been highlighted in blue. When an explanation has been offered this has been highlighted in green.

When developing my long arm over swing vault I decided to use repetition drills only. As this was the easier of my two vaults I knew as long as I took sufficient rest periods then repetition practice would be appropriate for me to work on perfecting my timing at take-off from the trampette. Repetition of the 'whole' skill was much easier for me and was the quickest way to help me refine my technique. I was already comfortable with my performance and used these drills simply to make fine adjustments to improve the overall aesthetic quality of my vault, for example extend my legs slightly earlier. This also allowed me to get immediate feedback from my coach. The actual vault takes seconds to perform and by repeating the action over and over again I became more confident and extremely consistent about all aspects of my performance; in particular my flight phase and my landings. The more I did the drill the better I got, I was then able to move the trampette slightly farther back to increase the complexity of the vault; it also made it more exciting to watch.

For my other vault the hand spring with half twist dismount I used gradual build up practice. I did this because of the complexity of the vault. I was not at the automatic stage of this vault and had problems with my half twist, to be honest this had much to do with my confidence as anything else. To ensure I made progress I would practise specific parts of the technique. I started performing the handspring on the floor, at this stage I worked on the power of my run up. I then added on the ½ twist. With no height drop from the apparatus to worry about I was able to concentrate more and take in the feedback offered by my coach. I then used the box but not at full height, I used extra crash mats to ensure I was safe. I had mis-timed my twist dismount a few times physical hurt myself so I felt the need for these extra mats. Once I had worked on sorting out my take-off from the trampette I was able to execute the movement with more height and so had more time in the air in which to perform the half twist. I finally moved onto the full height box but initially left the extra crash mats to give me confidence. Once I felt more consistent and confident I took the extra mats away and repeatedly practised the whole vault.

Both practices used were appropriate as they were specific to the complexity of the skill and matched my level of skill performance.

Examiners' feedback

This is a clear and detailed response. The writer understands about the information processing. Relevant and detailed information/diagram is given
to support points raised. The writer exhibits good critical thinking.   6/6

Now read the sample answer to part b

Note: when a description word/phrase has been used this has been highlighted in blue. When an explanation has been offered this has been highlighted in green.

The two factors that affected the development of my vaulting ability were feedback and confidence.

When practising my first vault I relied very much on kinaesthetic feedback. I was already comfortable with the skill and so could feel how well I was performing. I knew when my legs were not extended or whether I had managed to spot my landings accurately or not. I also received external feedback from my coach both verbal and visual, which also helped me to improve the overall quality of my technique. As the feedback was immediate I was able to take on the advice given and put it back into my whole performance. This type of feedback was important but had more of an impact on me as I practised my second vault. This was because this vault was much harder to perform. There were more sub-sections involved and therefore I needed diagnostic feedback from my coach to enable me to refine specific parts of my vault. I also needed the feedback frequently as I was not consistent and made errors at different sections. I felt closely related to feedback was my confidence. Due to the danger element of performing vaults it was crucial to be confident in myself so that I would not tense up and mistime my run-up or take-off. I had to be confident in my 'spotters' who were there to prevent me from falling. The repetitive nature of my practice increased my confidence very quickly and so I was able to make my performance look very relaxed and easy to perform. The gradual build up process reinforced my inner confidence; the more feedback I got the more confident I became and the fear of falling became less of an issue. My confidence also affected the aesthetic impression of my vault in that when I was unafraid I was able to get much higher in my flight phase and could also rotate more quickly on my half twist dismount. During competition my confidence had to be exceptionally positive so that I would not make mistakes. At this time although I was nervous because I was performing in front of a crowd I had to ensure I believed in myself and so make my vaults look more spectacular and so gain higher points from the judges.

Examiners' feedback

This is a clear and detailed response. The writer understands about the information processing. Relevant and detailed information/diagram is given to support points raised.
The writer exhibits good critical thinking.   6/6

Structure and strategy fundamentals

> **Key concept 1**
> The Structures, strategies and compositional elements that are fundamental to activities.

Remember in this **analysis area** you will be studying information that will help you to look at specific parts of your performance.

In this **key concept** you will learn about the fundamentals of structures, strategies and compositional considerations.

Within competitive individual and team activities there are certain fundamentals that, when applied, make performances more effective.

Understanding about the importance of these fundamentals (acquired knowledge), will enable you to plan, improvise and adapt performance(s) to match the immediate challenge (applied knowledge).

Key fundamentals

Let us examine the following key fundamentals.

Using space in attacking and defensive situations

To ensure game superiority, creating space and or denying space helps to manoeuvre and out-manoeuvre opponents. For example, in football the centre forward runs out to the wing, drawing his marker with him and creating space for a midfielder through the middle to run onto a long pass from defence.

Pressurising opponents in attacking and defensive situations

This could be forcing errors in certain situations, for example, in basketball, when defending your player you want to try and force them to dribble with their weak hand, hence making them make mistakes or forcing an error from them.

- Creating an overload situation, for example, trying to create a 3v2 situation or 2v1 when attacking when playing a fast break in basketball should allow an easy basket to be scored. The advantage of having an extra player should increase the chance of being successful.

Tempo of play, for example, varying the speed at which you decide to play can have an effect on the game or performance. For example, speed in attack. In tennis, you may decide to play a fast game by serving powerfully and going to net to volley and win points with smashes. Delay in defence – you may decide to play a slower speed of game by serving with more spin, staying on the baseline and using a variety of high returns and lobs against your opponent. Varying tempo offers an element of surprise.

Principles of individual and team play

These include width, depth, mobility, penetration, support and improvisation. Understanding about how to use, vary, change and adapt these principles are vital. It will make performances easier to deal with and will help exploit variations in formations and systems of play that opposition teams will apply. These principles can apply to both attacking and defensive situations.

- For example, in netball, width refers to the placement of a team's players with respect to the breadth of the court. Width, is important in attacking to split the opposition defence and prevent their working together. If the attack is spread out, the defence is spread out, creating more space for the attackers to move into to receive the ball and score points.

Depth refers to where players are in relation to the length of the court or area or being able to provide support to a specific set piece or play – for example, in rugby when the ball carrier is tackled, depth can be provided by players waiting to carry the ball forward into the next tackle and move up the field.

Improvisation refers to adapting or changing to the various performance situations that arise. Switching to another play or tactic allows a counteraction to the opposition or opponent's play. For example, in football a team could change from a 4–4–2 formation to a 4–5–1 formation as they were winning and wanted to be more defensive by having an extra player in midfield instead of having two attackers

- Mobility refers to keeping the players or ball on the move. This helps to control the immediate situation by keeping opponents guessing intent. It can also prevent them from reacting quickly leading to unforced errors or interceptions. For example, in basketball a motion offence is where players would pass and continually move to screen one another, moving defenders all over the court hoping to create a scoring opportunity for one of their players. Defenders are constantly being moved and dragged out of position
- Penetration refers to breaking through and getting ahead of an opponent or through a particular defence in a team game, thus creating opportunities to exploit to gain strategic advantage. For example, in rugby the wing forward can often pick up the ball from a scrum and break through the defensive line gaining ground for his team.

Structure and composition fundamentals

These fundamentals tend to be associated with the more creative activities. For example, dance, gymnastics, trampolining and synchronised swimming.

Important considerations

Design, form and style as compositional elements

Design in a performance refers to the arrangement of elements that make up the dance. For example, unity, variety, contrast, repetition, balance, pattern, the use of space and different motifs.

- Form in dance refers to the choreographical structure. Choreographic form may be defined as 'narrative' or 'pattern'. Narrative follows a story line (introduction, rising action, climax, resolution) and conveys specific meaning through that story. Pattern is structured around repetition of the elements of movement. Pattern choreographic forms may be based on the form of the music. Examples of pattern forms include: rondos and canons.

Style refers to the different origins/type of dance, for example, Scottish, Latin American, ethnic and ballroom.

- Developing motifs in performance. Motif development involves using a single movement or short movement stent phrase that is manipulated (e.g., by varying the elements of movement, by repetition, by using different body parts) to develop movement sequences for a dance.

- Using repetition, variation and contrast in performance. For example, when planning a floor routine a gymnast will consider some or all these fundamentals. Some skills require strong movements, such as a round-off or handspring in contrast to others requiring a lighter movement like a linking strep pattern. Similarly variation in routines are made by altering space/direction of movement and/or working at different levels and pathways.
- Using stimulus in performance refers to interpretation of a theme and or music content. For example, a particular theme like re-enacting emotions of a war requires strong, loud music.

Some further information is given in Structures, Strategies and Composition, **key concept** 2.

- Using space effectively in performance. For example, in gymnastics the performer wants to use as much space as possible in his/her floor routine to impress the judges. To use space effectively movements are selected and used in different directions at different levels with different body shapes. Travelling across the whole mat and involves the use of personal space (space around the body) as well as general space (space on the floor).
- Using creativity in performance refers to invention and/or composition to generate or express an idea to enhance a particular movement. For example, in gymnastics, a round-off, followed immediately with a straddle jump, followed immediately with a wolf jump or tumble combo with a cartwheel into a walkover is a good complex range of movement.

Top Tip

Remember these are just a few examples. If you have understood this **key concept** then you will be able to offer more examples from your own experiences.

Summary

Structures, strategies and compositional elements

Why has it been important to learn about this key concept?

Learning about this **key concept** has a range of benefits:

1. You will know more about fundamentals of structures and strategies.
2. You will know more about principles of play, both individual and team.
3. You will know more about the fundamentals of structures and compositional considerations.

For example, you will be able to consider:

*   the importance of space in performance
*   the importance of tempo of play
*   motifs in performance
*   the importance of repetition, variation and contrast in performance.

In the exam it is important that you are able to select one or more of each of the **structure and strategy fundamentals** and or one or more of the **structure and composition fundamentals** and be able to explain their importance when using a particular structure, strategy or composition.

Using these strategies in the exam

Remember, in your exam you may be asked to demonstrate your understanding of this **key concept** by *recalling* the information.

In this instance, you could be asked the following:

*   Structures, strategies or compositions are based on a number of key fundamentals, for example:
    *   using space effectively
    *   developing motifs in performance
    *   the importance of creativity
    *   pressure in performance.

Select two from the list above and explain their importance when applying a chosen structure, strategy or composition.

Exam Success

Look back at the commands words on page 9.

Quick Task

Select a **structure, strategy or composition** you have used in class. Explain the importance of space when applying this **structure, strategy or composition**. Try to give examples that will support your answer.

Keep this as part of your study notes. It will help you to recall information more efficiently.

Improving your exam technique

Let us examine a past paper question and response. This time you are looking at an explanation as to why the two key fundamentals selected are important when applying the chosen structure, strategy or composition.

6 marks

Sample question, answer and feedback

Question

Structures, strategies or compositions are based on a number of key principles/fundamentals.
For example:

- speed in attack
- width/depth/mobility
- using repetition, variation and contrast
- the importance of creativity.

Choose two, either from your course or from the list above and **explain** their importance when applying a structure, strategy or composition.

6 marks

Now read the sample answer

Note: where an explanation has been offered this has been highlighted in green.

For example the importance of creativity. The activity is tennis and the strategy was to play a serve and volley game When applying my strategy it is important to be creative. I need to create a variety of options in response to the changing circumstances in a game otherwise my opponent will know exactly what I am going to do. They will be prepared and will be able to respond in a particular way. In a tennis game it is about ball placement and this will depend on the position of my opponent and the space available. Doing the unexpected creates an element of surprise, catching my opponent off guard. This could be playing a drop volley at net rather than a normal drive volley. Being creative also leads to me being unpredictable, for example taking the pace off the ball when I serve or serving to my opponents backhand – this can upset your opponent. Being creative adds flair to your game and can create winners from a difficult position and can win you points. I could do this also by disguising a shot or direction of the ball, trying to wrong-foot my opponent by playing a drop shot instead of a volley at the net when my opponent is at the back of the court after a service return. I could also play a heavy top spin on my second serve. Being creative can also provide different options, often leading to mistakes from my opponent.

The second principle is tempo/speed in play .When applying my strategy, tempo/speed is important. I need to vary the speed, depending on the circumstances, to be effective. My service could be delivered at a fast pace or slower for tactical reason. It could depend on the position my opponent stands in to receive the serve or where they are when they return the ball. If they are at the back of the court I am more likely to take the pace off the ball or if I find my opponent is good at passing me as I am at the net after my serve I might stay back and try to play from baseline and hit the ball with pace from side to side. I could also introduce variation in tempo of my strategy by varying the depth, pace and using spin or slice in my serve to give me time to get into net. I want to be able to control each rally so the speed and tempo is important. Varying the speed/tempo I play will not allow my opponent to get into a rhythm and dictate play and will also make my opponent think about each shot and hopefully lead to mistakes being made.

Top Tip

Practise giving this amount of detail in your answers and you are well on your way to a good pass.

Examiners' feedback

This is a clear and detailed response. A detailed explanation is given as to the importance of each fundamental selected.

The writer offers good critical thinking. 6/6

Roles and relationships

> **Key concept 2**
> Identification of strengths and weaknesses in performance in terms of: roles and relationships, formations, tactical and design elements, choreography and composition.

In this key concept you will be studying information that will help you to look at roles and relationships, formations, tactical or design elements, choreography and composition.

Game effectiveness depends on how successfully you fulfil specific role(s). Within each role certain responsibilities are associated with it. Carrying out these responsibilities ensures that your team plays effectively.

Before adopting a particular role it is important to recognise the following:

- The responsibilities that go with that role for example, a hooker in rugby has to be able to win the ball at scrums, be accurate in throwing into line outs, put pressure on the opposing hooker in scrums and be able to win possession in second phase play.
- The individual strengths and weaknesses, for example, in basketball, as a guard your strengths might be your accurate passing, good dribbling skills or ability to beat your opponent, whereas your weaknesses may be your rebounding because of your height. Other considerations may be linked to physique or fitness.
- The demands of the role, for example, a striker in football must have good strength to hold off defenders and shield the ball, quick reactions in and around the penalty box, be able to link together with other players, have good close control and have a good level of physical fitness.

Think about the activities you have done on your course. What role did you play? What were the demands and what were your strengths and weaknesses?

Once these factors have been considered then a relevant structure, strategy or composition can be selected to meet the specific performance demands.

For example:

- basketball – a fast break/zones/1–3–1/horse shoe offence in/man/man defence
- football – 4–2–4 or 4–3–3 or 3–5–2
- badminton – front–back–side–side
- gymnastics – particular sequence/routine
- volleyball – court rotation
- hockey – penalty corner

In context, examine the considerations made:

In tennis, I used a serve volley strategy. I would serve fast and hard to my opponent, follow my serve, get into net and position quickly, use a volley to win point, from opponents' return.

Top Tip

Make sure you are able to describe the structure, strategy or composition you have used in your course.

In basketball when you have a tall team who can win rebounds it is better for you to play zone defence. This can link-in to using the guards to play a fast break. They are quick down the court and have good ball handling skills. Here you are taking into account the responsibilities and the strengths of particular players.

Note: for a team to work effectively all players must cooperate, communicate and carry out their roles and responsibilities to the highest level possible. This also means being able to adapt/change quickly to meet the varying game demands.

Formations

This means the way a team lines up.

Important learning points

- The structure of relevant systems of play in selected activities. For example, 4–4–2 in football or 4–3–3 in hockey or 2–1–2 zone in basketball or W formation in volleyball.
- The benefits and limitations of various systems of play; each formation will have particular advantages and disadvantages. Consider the following examples:

STRUCTURE
2–1–2 zone in basketball 

ADVANTAGE/BENEFITS	DISADVANTAGES/LIMITATIONS
• Protects inside against a team of good drivers and post players. • Is effective against poor outside shooters. • Easy to learn. • Protects players in foul trouble. • Effective against screens and cutting. • Less tiring.	• Can be difficult to defend against good outside shooter. • Can be susceptible against a good fast break team. • Easier for opponents to maintain lead at end of game. • Can be vulnerable to a quick passing team. • Weak against a team who can penetrate zone.

Consider the advantages/benefits and disadvantages/limitation of your selected structure, strategy or composition.

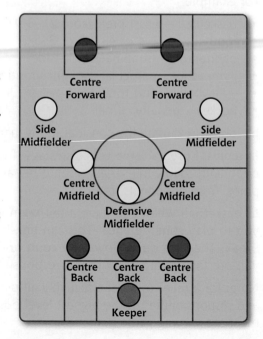

- The need to co-operate and support others in various systems of play. In any formation it is important for players to support and cooperate together. This will allow better teamwork and ensure the formation works more effectively, for example, in football 3–5–2 the defenders in the back three must co-operate and support one another. If a long ball is played by the opposition they must make sure they are not square with one another nor too far apart. They can avoid this by talking to one another and moving closer together. Also if one goes to ball the other two cover across to plug the gaps and support the defender going to ball.

Think about an example of how you could support and co-operate in an activity in your course.

- The ability to pre-plan strategies to suit the demands of play.

When you plan to use various strategies there are many factors you should consider. This is done beforehand (game plan) to ensure that when unpredictable circumstances appear you are able to adapt quickly and cope with pressures.

Your choice of structure, strategy or composition will depend on many factors.

- Strengths and weaknesses of your own team.
- Strengths and weaknesses of the opposition, in particular strengths of individual players within the structure, strategy or composition.
- Experience of players in the team or opposition.
- Previous results.
- How long you can apply the structure, strategy or composition.
- Current score in the game.
- Time point in the game, weather or ground conditions.
- Amount of space to perform in, type of music, apparatus selected.

Tactical and design elements

Tactics

When you carry out a particular strategy you will apply certain tactics to achieve your goal. A tactic is a plan to attain your goal. Tactics will vary according to the strategy you carry out and could vary or be adapted depending on various circumstances. Adaptations and changes will be addressed in **key concept** 3.

When adopting to use tactics it is important to:

- Identify and exploit your opponent's weaknesses. For example, in tennis, having played against my opponent previously, I knew his backhand was weak so I made sure I served to that side. This often led to a poor return on his part As I had forced my opponent out-wide in the service area I could often volley his poor return into the open court away from him to gain an outright winner.

- Maximise strengths within the chosen structure or strategy. For example, in volleyball we had a very tall spiker who could jump high and had an accurate and powerful spike which won us many points. We tried as often as possible to use his strengths and set the ball up for him to spike by adopting a strategy which put him in the spiking position as often as possible.

The second example considers using a particular player suited for a particular role. Other factors could be: type of opposition; attack/defence being applied by the team or opposition; time restrictions in a game after a particular time or situation in an activity; ground or weather conditions; prior or previous knowledge of opponent's previous results.

The key elements of overall design/form/style

Design

This is the arrangement of elements that make up a dance or a floor sequence in gymnastics. For example, in gymnastics it will involve linking various movements together and using the space on the mat.

Form

This is the way in which the choreography of a dance is structured. The dance could follow a storyline throughout or follow a set of different patterns that are often repeated. Examples of these include canons, groups performing the same theme or sequence but beginning at different times so they overlap; rondos, where movement A is followed by movement B, then repeated, then followed by a different movement C then A is repeated again (ABABCA, etc); themes and variations, where a movement is performed and then repeated with various changes, for example, faster or slower but still maintaining its structure and sequence.

Style

This involves different styles of dance, for example, Scottish, Latin American, ethnic and ballroom. Also within each certain type of dance there may be various styles for example, Latin American includes Salsa, Rumba, Calpyso and Merengue.

Developing motifs, phrases and themes

A motif is a pattern or theme that is repeated often enough in the performance to make it a significant or dominant feature. A motif is similar to theme or melody in a musical composition. Motif development involves using a single movement or short movement phrase that is manipulated (for example, by varying the elements of movement, by repetition, by using different body parts) to develop movement sequences for a dance. Phrases are motifs that join together.

Ways of linking different elements together

When performing a dance sequence or gymnastic routine a series of movements are linked together. To make the performance more aesthetically pleasing, different elements are explored.

These could include:

- the use of space involving how the body moves using different pathways
- different body actions including gestures and body movements; dynamic/sustained
- different levels: high/low
- changes of direction
- different timing of movements; fast/slow. often dictated by theme or music tempo.

Choreography and composition

When considering choreography and composition, the following factors are important.

*   Timing, precision and improvisation in performance. For example, 'My actions in my dance had to fit precisely with my choice of music. The timing had to be exact – my footwork, steps and jumps had to be timed and precise so that I always arrived where I intended to and for maximum visual impact on the audience.'
*   Sensitivity and expression within performance. For example, 'I had to instil emotion, and feelings into my dance by interpreting the music effectively, thus conveying to the spectators the mood and intent. Often a strong head gesture or strong eye gaze energised the mood.'

Summary

Identification of strengths and weaknesses

Why has it been important to learn about this key concept?

Learning about this **key concept** has a range of benefits:

1. You will know more about the importance of roles and relationships.
2. You will know about formations.
3. You will have gained knowledge of tactical or design elements.
4. You will know the importance of various features of choreography and composition.

For example, you will be able to consider:

- the demands and responsibilities of particular roles
- the benefits and limitations of various formations
- ways of linking different elements together
- the importance of timing, precision, and mood in performance.

In your exam it is important that you are able to describe a structure, strategy or composition you have worked on and be able to describe how you collected data on it. You must be able to show both acquired and applied knowledge of one of the following:

- roles and relationships
- formations
- tactical or design elements
- choreography and composition.

Using these strategies in the exam

Remember, in your exam you may be asked to demonstrate your understanding of this **key concept** by *recalling* the information.

In this instance, you could be asked to:

- describe the role you performed when applying a structure, strategy or composition
- explain the benefits and limitations that you have to take into account in your selected structure, strategy or composition.

Alternatively you could be asked to demonstrate how you were able to make use of this acquired knowledge. For example, you could be asked to:

- discuss some of the decisions you had to make to ensure you carried out your role effectively when applying your selected structure, strategy or composition
- discuss the strengths a performer needs to successfully implement in the selected structure, strategy or composition
- choose one of the following and explain their importance when applying your selected structure, strategy or composition.

Exam Success

Look back at the commands words on page 9.

Quick Task

From one of the areas of roles and relationships, formations, tactical or design elements and choreography and composition, note one or more bullet points and explain their importance in a structure, strategy or composition you have been using in an activity in your course.

Improving your exam technique

Let us examine a past paper question and response. This time you are looking at a discussion of factors you would take into account before selecting a structure, strategy or composition. This links into the ability to pre-plan strategies to meet the demands of play.

Sample question, answer and feedback

Question

Discuss the factors you would take into consideration when selecting a structure, strategy or composition.

6 marks

Now read the sample answer

Note: when a discussion word/phrase has been used this has been highlighted in yellow.

The activity chosen is basketball.

When considering selecting a particular strategy I would take into account first of all the strengths and weaknesses of the opposition that we are playing against. If we had played them previously I would have some idea of what they were like as a team and would know what players were good or who was weak at particular things. This may then allow me to decide upon a particular strategy that could exploit these weaknesses or counteract their strategy. For example, if I knew the opposition had good outside shooters when playing basketball I would decide to play half court man-to-man to nullify this and force them to drive to the basket.

I would also consider the strengths and weaknesses of my own team and in particular certain players who may be able to carry out specialist roles with the activity. For example when playing basketball in man/man defence, who is my best defender, who could win us turnovers as a team or force most mistakes from the opposition? Who is my concern if a player fouls and do we have a good substitute should that happen in a game?

I also would take into account the fitness level of our team and how long we could carry out the strategy before fatigue set in and our play started to deteriorate. The score and time in an actual game are factors to take into account. If we are losing and we are in the last few minutes of a game then we might decide to change or select a strategy that would be effective at this stage of the game and possibly let us win in the final few minutes. Finally the previous results of the opposition, if we had played them before, will be taken into account. I would know what had happened and how we won or lost the match and that may have an influence on what strategy I might use.

Top Tip

Practise giving this amount of detail in your answers and you are well on your way to a good pass.

Examiners' feedback

This is a clear and detailed response. The writer offers good discussion of the factors to be taken into account before selecting a structure, strategy or composition. The writer exhibits good analytical thinking.

6/6

Gathering information to aid decision making

> **Key concept 3**
> Information processing, problem solving and decision making when working to develop and improve performance.

In this **key concept** you will learn about making decisions about the structure, strategy or composition you are using by processing information and problem solving. This will allow you where necessary to adapt or change the structure, strategy or composition.

Gathering useful information

We can use information on team/individual performance to make decisions when developing, monitoring and evaluating performance.

To ensure effective performances, information is often gathered beforehand, which helps you to plan and further develop your performance. By processing this information, effective decisions are taken to improve performance by considering various factors:

Previous knowledge

This is often gathered from statistics, video footage, self reflection etc.

For example, 'In basketball our stats showed that the previous time we played our rivals they always played a zone defence that was difficult to break down, and we were forced to shoot from outside, which we were not particularly successful at.'

- Decision: 'We decided to play fast break as often as possible so we could attack before the defence could set up their zone.'

Strengths and weaknesses of the team

We can take an overview of team abilities etc. For example, 'In rugby our team had very strong powerful forwards who were very good at driving forward and maintaining possession, especially winning the ball by rucks and mauls.'

- Decision: 'We decided to play a tight game by keeping the ball with the forwards as much as possible.'

Ground/weather conditions/venue

These external factors often featured in a prematch report etc. For example, 'In football, it was a very windy day, with the wind blowing straight down the park. This meant that we would play with and into the wind in different halves of the game.'

- Decision: 'If we were playing against the wind we tried to keep the ball low and play to feet and keep a high formation in defence.'

Strengths and weaknesses of the opposition

These are often gathered from statistics, video footage. For example, 'In hockey, the team we were playing were very successful at set plays at penalty corners and often scored against us.'

- Decision: 'We tried not to give away infringes in the circle thus preventing penalty corners.'

Using relevant information

Good performers will also be aware of information internally assessed during performance; (processed as a result of 'scanning' and 'internalising exactly what is happening'). As a result of reacting to game cues and different types of stimuli, performers can easily adapt/change the selection and/or application of skills, techniques, strategy or composition to cope better with the immediate challenge.

Selecting the relevant information from the irrelevant information on display to ensure you are effective takes years of practice. Consider some of the following factors that challenge your ability to process information and more importantly to make appropriate decisions at the appropriate time.

Time

Elite performers, whilst applying skills, will be aware of external factors such as time. For example, 'In basketball, we were six points ahead with 1 minute to play and had possession of the ball.'

- Decision: 'We decided to run the clock down by keeping possession and forcing our opponents to somehow get the ball back.'

Score in the game

For example, 'In football we were losing 1–0 and trying to get an equalizer.'

- Decision: 'We pushed our tall centre half into attack in the hope he would win headers and maybe score or set up chances for our forwards.'

Actions that happen during game/performance

For example, 'When playing badminton I noticed my opponent was poor on their backhand side and made many errors.'

- Decision: 'I tried to force my opponent onto their backhand as often as possible.'

Decisions during performance

During performance it is important to continually:

- Be perceptive. For example, 'In basketball I noticed the player I was marking always used her right hand when dribbling. She was not confident using her left hand and often made mistake when she was forced to use this hand so I tried as much as possible to force her to use her left.'
- Be creative. For example, 'In football when taking a free kick just outside our opponents' box, three players would line up to take it. One player would run over ball, one would pass it short, and the other would shoot for goal.'
- Make effective decisions under pressure. For example, 'As a goalkeeper in hockey at a penalty corner, I had to decide what course of action I had to take, whether to stay in goal or rush out to block the shooter. I decided to rush out. I did this and blocked the shot and prevented a goal.'
- Exercise effective solutions. For example, 'When playing tennis my opponent liked to serve and volley so I decided to try and use a lob as often as possible and force him to the back of the court. I also tried to return the serve to his feet, which made it very difficult for him to volley.'

You will also cover this information in more detail in Skills and Techniques, **key concept** 1.

Be constantly 'on the ball'

Finally, when applying your structure, strategy or composition you will be faced with many ever-changing situations. To be effective as a team or individual, responses must be evident.

This may involve adapting/changing or refining your structure, strategy or composition.

As an example of changing in response to a situation, 'In basketball we were playing a 2–1–2 zone and the opposition had good outside shooters and were scoring frequently. We changed to half court man/man defence to stop them. This led to less successful shots as they were under more pressure and had less time to shoot. This forced them to try and drive to basket They made more mistakes and scored less baskets as they were poor at driving to basket. As a result we won more turnovers and could attack more.'

An example of refining your structure, strategy or composition could be in football, 'We played a 4–4–2 formation. We found when attacking that all four players in midfield would be up the park supporting the forwards. When the attack broke down, the opposition often broke quickly and our midfield were slow to get back and our defence was under pressure. We decided to refine by having one player holding in midfield in front of the back four, one midfield supporting the strikers and the other two in middle to move back and forward as necessary. This lead to a more balanced attack and defence and allowed us to prevent the opposition breaking quickly as our holding midfielder was able to delay attack and allow others to get back to defend.'

In both examples above, changing tactics hopefully lead to an effective solution being carried out and a more effective structure, strategy or composition being applied. This has involved:

- information being processed
- decision making
- problem solving
- working to develop and improve performance.

Summary

Information Processing

Why has it been important to learn about this key concept?

Learning about this **key concept** has a range of benefits:

1. You will know about using information to develop, monitor and evaluate performance.
2. You will know the importance of adapting/changing and refining structures, strategies and composition.
3. You will be able to link this understanding to make sense of other **key concepts** as you study the other **analysis areas**.

For example, you will be able to consider:

- the importance of making decisions under pressure
- how to adapt/change and refine structures, strategies and composition.

Top Tip

Remember these are just a few examples. If you have understood this **key concept** then you will be able to offer more examples from your own experiences.

Using these strategies in the exam

Remember, in your exam you may be asked to demonstrate your understanding of this **key concept** by *recalling* the information.

In this instance there is a considerable depth about what you may be asked, for example:

You could be asked to

- discuss the factors you would take into consideration when selecting a structure, strategy or composition
- having adapted or changed the structure, strategy or composition, explain how you would evaluate its effectiveness.

Alternatively you could be asked to demonstrate how you were able to make use of this acquired knowledge. For example, you could be asked to:

- Briefly describe a situation where you had to adapt or change the structure, strategy or composition. Discuss why the changes or adaptations made your performance more effective.

Exam Success

Look back at the commands words on page 9.

Quick Task

Think how you gathered information on your structure, strategy or composition. What decisions were you faced with when you decided to select this? How would you adapt/change or refine this structure, strategy or composition?

Keep this as part of your study notes. It will help you to recall information more efficiently.

Improving your exam technique

Let us examine a past paper question and response.

This time you are looking at a description and discussion of related facts for 6 marks. Firstly, to help you make sense of how the examiner is testing why you would change or adapt a structure, strategy or composition, you have an opportunity to *read* parts a) and b) of the same question before *answering* part c).

Sample questions, answers and feedback

Question

a) **Discuss** the factors you would take into consideration when selecting a structure, strategy or composition.　　6 marks
b) **Describe** in detail a structure, strategy or composition that you have used.　　4 marks
c) **Briefly describe** a situation where you had to adapt or change the structure, strategy or composition in part (b). **Discuss** why these changes or adaptations made your performance more effective.　　6 marks

Now read the sample answer to part c

Note: when a description word/phrase has been used this has been highlighted in blue. When an discussion has been offered this has been highlighted in yellow.

When we were playing against another school they became familiar with our fast break as we tended to use the same break all the time. They knew exactly what the ball handler was going to do each time they reached the top of the key and as soon as the ball handler made the pass the forward was put under pressure and often was stopped in their drive to the basket, causing the break to stop. This prevented us from scoring baskets and we had to try another play.

We decided to change our options we could use in the break. The same initial parts of the break were carried, but as soon as the ball carrier reached the half-way circle they now passed the ball early to one of the forwards at the side who then dribbled for a few strides and then passed the ball diagonally across the key to the other clear forward who had an easy drive to the basket to score a lay-up. This caused an element of surprise and caused the defence to be caught unawares. It also meant as the ball was passed earlier at the half-way line there was less time for the defence to get back and allowed our team more time and space to drive to the basket. We also added another option from this break where the forward who received the diagonal pass could fake to drive and reverse the ball back to the ball carrier who had now reached a position just inside the key for a close jump shot to the basket. Again this caused an element of surprise. It now meant that we had various options we could use and the defence could not predict which break we were going to use. This meant that the fast break worked successfully more often and we scored more baskets.

Top Tip

Practise giving this amount of detail in your answers and you are well on your way to a good pass.

Examiners' feedback

This is a clear and detailed response. A brief detailed description is given of a situation where it was necessary to change/adapt the structure, strategy or composition. A detailed discussion is given as to how the performance was more effective. The writer offers good critical thinking.　　6/6

Study guide

How do you structure your study time?

For many of you, study means going through your notes and making yet more notes! Whilst this may be necessary, if you do not practise how to *select* and *use* that information, you are neglecting an important part of how you are going to be ultimately assessed.

Let us help you to plan and think more logically about your study preparation – this should avoid the temptation to write 'all you know' about a topic.

- Study regularly and in fairly short intervals with breaks in between - this will keep you alert and avoid boredom.
- Organise your study in a logical order; remember you need to consider your other subject commitments too! (Refer to your SQA timetable to help you prioritise your time.)
- Focus on tasks, not time.
- Go through your notes and highlight/underline key points – this will refresh your memory from your class notes.
- Spend an hour going through an analysis chapter – this will help you to recall material and select from it.
- Find a sample question and answer it – time yourself as this will help you not to write too much for one answer.

Using this approach consistently should pay huge dividends as it is more effective than merely reading your notes. Importantly, it will help prevent a stressful build up to your exams; in particular your Physical Education examination.

Remember – cramming is not fun and never works.

Something to consider

In *failing to prepare* you are *preparing to fail*.

And finally the exam itself!

Most of this advice is relevant for all your subjects.

Be consistent in your exam strategy

Keep calm! If you have been active in your learning and have worked to consolidate your understanding, you will have little difficulty in remembering it.

- Before you start writing, read the whole question paper first. Read questions right through before you choose; perhaps the second part of the question asks for something you do not know about and therefore you would be better to make another choice.
- Select the three questions that you know most about (refer to all parts a–d). While you may be able to tailor what you know to answer a given question, it is important to resist the temptation to answer the question you hoped would be asked, or to write down everything you know that is vaguely related to the question.
- Plan the order you will answer them in, for example, completing the analysis area that you used for your NAB is often a good idea.
- Underline or highlight the command words and important phrases.
- Be aware of your write up time for each of the three questions – share out your time effectively!
- Try to leave some time at the end of the exam so that you can check your answers over. A little time spent checking can sometime save you quite a lot of marks and could make the difference between an A, B and a C grade.

Finally...

Ask yourself – having put a full stop at the end of a sentence – 'Do I really want the reader to stop reading *or* is there any more information I could add?' In most instances there is always information you could add to support your answer.

Life skills

'Wisdom is not a product of schooling but of the lifelong attempt to acquire it.'

Albert Einstein

Education is about gaining knowledge and perhaps, more importantly, how you apply this knowledge. In most instances knowledge gained is transferable. In other words, what you learn in one subject can help you to achieve success in another. Always try to **make the link** and challenge your mind to enquire, find solutions and answer queries.

The most critical factor in your life is self-belief. The way you feel affects the way you think and the way you think affects the way you feel. Endeavour to be a disciplined and positive thinker.

Being involved in sport prepares you for life's challenges and will be invaluable to you later in life.

One final thought...

'Nowhere is the mind–body connection more dramatically visible than in competitive sport. Mind, body, spirit, feelings, emotions are all part of the same continuum of life. There is and can be no separation.

Loehr